# Naval War College Style Manual And Classification Guide

# Contents

# Naval War College Style Manual And Classification Guide

*by* U.S. Naval War College

*from* Nimble Books LLC: The AI Lab for Book-Lovers

~ Fred Zimmerman, Editor ~

*Humans and AI making books richer, more diverse, and more surprising.*

## Publishing Information

- (c) 2024 Nimble Books LLC
- ISBN: 978-1-60888-317-2

## AI-generated Bibliographic Keywords

Naval War College Style Manual; NWC Style Guide; Naval War College Classification Guide; Research Paper Formatting Guide; Military Writing Style; Naval Writing Style; Classified Document Marking; Security Classification for Research; NWC Research Paper Submission; DTIC Submission; Report Documentation Page; Don ISPR; Executive Order 12958; Security Classification Guidelines; Military Research Guidelines.

## Publisher's Notes

This annotated edition illustrates the capabilities of the AI Lab for Book-Lovers to add context and ease-of-use to manuscripts. It includes several types of abstracts, building from simplest to more complex: TLDR (one word), ELI5, TLDR (vanilla), Scientific Style, and Action Items; essays to increase viewpoint diversity, such as Grounds for Dissent, Red Team Critique, and MAGA Perspective; and Notable Passages and Nutshell Summaries for each page.

# Abstracts

## TL;DR (one word)

References.

## Explain It To Me Like I'm Five Years Old

Okay, imagine you have a big box of toys. Some toys are for everyone to play with, like your teddy bear or toy car. But some toys are special and only certain people can play with them, like a special action figure that you need to be very careful with.

Now, when grown-ups write important papers or books, sometimes they include information that everyone can read, like stories or facts about what happened in history. But other times, they have special information that only certain people can see.

## Simple Summary

The Naval War College Style Manual and Classification Guide is an indispensable resource for writers engaged in scholarly research and analysis. This comprehensive manual provides detailed guidance on formatting, documentation, and security classification of research papers, ensuring clarity, consistency, and adherence to professional standards. The manual emphasizes the importance of proper citation and documentation to avoid plagiarism and to facilitate reader comprehension. It also includes a selective list of commonly used publishers and their acceptable abbreviations, further streamlining the research process.

## Action Items

*Retrospective, as if reading the document when it was written.*

It looks like you're dealing with a variety of sources, including books, congressional reports, and classified documents. Here are some suggested action items to help you manage and organize your research:

**Organize Your Sources:**

- Create a bibliography or reference list to keep track of all your sources.
- Use a citation management tool like EndNote, Zotero, or Mendeley to help organize and format your references.

**Classified Documents Handling:**

- Ensure you follow all guidelines for handling classified documents, including not referencing their classified status in public documents.

## Key Takeaways

- This manual provides a comprehensive guide for preparing, classifying, and distributing research papers at the Naval War College.
- The goal is to ensure high-quality scholarship that is properly documented, formatted, and secured according to national security regulations.
- The manual emphasizes the importance of adhering to specific style and formatting guidelines for clarity and consistency.
- The manual also highlights the importance of accurately citing sources and understanding the implications of using classified material.

## Memory Aids

*The traditional sober-minded "parts of the book" are useful for diligent researchers, but they aren't necessarily suited to the needs of a more impatient modern generation of readers. Here are some mnemonics, a ditty, and a mash-up to help you retain the key points.*

### Mnemonic (speakable)

Notes, Bibliography, Classification: This helps remember the main sections of the guide.

### Ditty

*to the tune of "Pop Goes the Weasel"*:

'Double-space your text,

Footnotes at the bottom.

Bibliography's next,

With sources in a row.

If classified it's true,

Follow the rules, you see.

NWC wants it right,

To keep our secrets free.'

### Mash-up

Top Secret Research: The Dewey Decimal System Meets "Mission: Impossible" (This combines the topic of classified research with the structure of libraries and a popular spy franchise.)

# Viewpoints

*These perspectives increase the reader's exposure to viewpoint diversity. No endorsement of any particular view is intended.*

## Grounds for Dissent

A member of the organization responsible for the document might have principled, substantive reasons to dissent from the report due to various plausible concerns. Here are detailed reasons why such dissent might occur:

Ethical Concerns Regarding Classification

**Transparency vs. Secrecy**: The report might excessively rely on classified information, which could hinder transparency and accountability. An individual might believe that the public has a right to be fully informed about certain aspects of defense and government activities and that the current level of classification unjustifiably restricts this knowledge.

**Misuse of Classification**: There could be a belief that classification is being used not for genuine security purposes but to avoid scrutiny and hide incompetence, mistakes, or controversial decisions. This misuse could undermine public trust in the government and its institutions.

Strategic and Doctrinal Disagreements

**Doctrine Development**: As referenced by James J. Tritten's work on naval perspectives for military doctrine development, there could be substantive disagreements over the strategic doctrines proposed. A member might feel that the doctrines are either outdated, overly aggressive, or not aligned with current geopolitical realities.

**Resource Allocation**: The report might advocate for resource allocation that a member believes is misguided. For example, emphasizing certain military capabilities or technologies at the expense of others might be seen as strategically flawed.

Policy and Decision-Making Critiques

**Historical Decision-Making Critique**: Drawing from historical analyses like those of Henry A. Kissinger and other cited works, a member might dissent based on different interpretations of past decisions. They might argue that historical precedents are being misinterpreted or selectively used to justify current policies.

**Need for Organizational Change**: Referring to the 1985 Defense Organization report, there might be dissatisfaction with the proposed organizational structures or reforms. A member might believe that the suggested changes either do not go far enough or are misdirected.

Legal and Procedural Concerns

**Legal Compliance**: There may be concerns about the legality of certain recommendations or actions described in the report. This includes adherence to domestic laws, international treaties, and conventions, such as the Law of the Sea debates mentioned in John B. Breaux's statement.

**Procedural Accuracy**: The report's methodology might be seen as flawed or biased. If the research methods, data collection, or analysis are perceived as inadequate, this could form a basis for dissent.

Ethical Implications of Military Actions

**Moral and Ethical Implications**: The report might propose actions that a member finds ethically questionable. This could involve the use of certain weapons, engagement in conflicts that are seen as unjust, or policies that disproportionately affect civilian populations.

Organizational Culture and Values

**Internal Culture**: There might be a belief that the report perpetuates an internal culture that is resistant to necessary change. A member might feel that the report does not adequately address issues of diversity, inclusion, or evolving military ethics.

Impact on Civil-Military Relations

**Civil-Military Relations**: Recommendations in the report might be seen as damaging to the relationship between civilian oversight bodies and the military. If the report is perceived to undermine civilian control or oversight, it could be a significant point of contention.

In summary, dissenting views might arise from concerns about transparency, ethical use of classification, strategic and doctrinal disagreements, legal and procedural issues, moral implications of proposed actions, and the overall impact on organizational culture and civil-military relations. Each of these areas reflects deep-seated principles and substantive considerations that could lead a member to formally dissent from the report.

## MAGA Perspective

*In an increasingly polarized market for English-language books, it must be assumed that readers will come into contact with views of the topic that are deeply skeptical of conventional wisdom.*

What a colossal waste of taxpayer dollars! This document, with its endless citations and bureaucratic jargon, is nothing short of a disgrace. It's filled to the brim with references to hearings, reports, and documents that were probably concocted behind closed doors by unelected officials and career politicians. The deep state loves to bury important decisions in layers of classified nonsense, making it impossible for the average American to understand what's really going on. They claim it's about national security, but it's more about keeping We the People in the dark.

Look at this nonsense about the "Law of the Sea." John B. Breaux and his highfalutin statements in front of Congress are nothing more than pandering to internationalists. This is the kind of global governance that the UN pushes and the Democrats drool over. They want us to believe that international laws should take precedence over our Constitution and our national interests. It's just another way to chip away at our freedom, our sovereignty, and our right to govern ourselves without foreign interference.

And don't get me started on the classified documents. They conveniently classify anything that might actually inform the public about what's really going on. It's a tactic straight out of the authoritarian playbook. Keep the populace uninformed and distracted. When will it end? When will we have a government that actually believes in transparency and accountability? The only way to drain this swamp is to elect leaders who will tear down these walls of secrecy and return power to the people. The MAGA movement stands for transparency, sovereignty, and the dismantling of the deep state—a far cry from the bureaucratic nightmare laid out in this document.

# Five Most Important Passages

Here are five key direct quotations from the Naval War College Style Manual and Classification Guide, chosen for their importance to the overall message of the document:

- "Information classified by DON Original Classification Authorities (OCAs) shall be declassified as soon as it no longer meets the standards for classification in the interest of national security." (Chapter IV, Paragraph 4-1)
  - This emphasizes the importance of declassification and the principle of minimizing the duration of classification.
- "The author's name should include given name, family name, and middle initial(s). Titles such as doctor, professor, or captain, together with the author's position and degrees held, should be omitted; titles of nobility before given names or initials, however, should be included." (Chapter III, Page 11)
  - This clarifies the correct way to present author information in notes and bibliographies, avoiding extraneous details.
- "Mark (stamp, print, or permanently affix with a sticker or tape) the face and back cover, top and bottom center, of all classified documents to show the highest overall classification level of the information they contain." (Chapter IV, Paragraph 6-3)
  - This instruction underscores the crucial need for clear and consistent marking of classified documents to ensure proper handling and security.
- "When determining the duration of classification, choose one of the following three declassification instructions: (Whenever possible, select the declassification instruction that will result in the shortest duration of classification.)" (Chapter IV, Page 43)
  - This excerpt highlights the principle of limiting the duration of classification as much as possible, consistent with national security requirements.
- "Papers prepared for the Naval War College are considered to belong to the College." (Chapter V, Page 50)
  - This establishes the ownership and rights of the Naval War College over student papers, research reports, and prize essays, setting the foundation for their distribution and deposit policies.
  - These quotations are chosen for their direct impact on how to write, cite, classify, and handle research papers produced by the Naval War College. They exemplify the balance between scholarly integrity, proper attribution, and national security concerns.

# Five Striking Passages

Here are five striking, insightful, and well-phrased passages from the document, excluding the previously mentioned five quotations:

*"Because potential readers rely heavily on abstracts to help them cull from a large menu those papers that they will read in their entirety, abstracts tend to be marketing devices." (Chapter I, Page 1)*

*"The general rule: 'When in doubt, provide a citation,' applies." (Chapter III, Page 9)*

*"Mark each portion (e.g., title, section, part, paragraph, or subparagraph) of a classified document to show its classification level. This requirement eliminates doubt as to which portions of a document are classified." (Chapter IV, Paragraph 6-5)*

*"Subjects or titles shall be unclassified for identification and reference purposes." (Chapter IV, Paragraph 6-6)*

*"All newly generated unclassified technical documents must bear one of the distribution statements described in Exhibit 8A of the DON ISPR." (Chapter IV, Paragraph 8-8)*

These passages are notable for their clarity, precision, and insightful observations about the nature of academic writing, security protocols, and the need for responsible information dissemination.

# NAVAL WAR COLLEGE

# *Style Manual and Classification Guide*

August 2000

<table>
<tr><td colspan="3" align="center">**Report Documentation Page**</td><td>*Form Approved*<br>*OMB No. 0704-0188*</td></tr>
<tr><td colspan="4">Public reporting burden for the collection of information is estimated to average 1 hour per response, including the time for reviewing instructions, searching existing data sources, gathering and maintaining the data needed, and completing and reviewing the collection of information. Send comments regarding this burden estimate or any other aspect of this collection of information, including suggestions for reducing this burden, to Washington Headquarters Services, Directorate for Information Operations and Reports, 1215 Jefferson Davis Highway, Suite 1204, Arlington VA 22202-4302. Respondents should be aware that notwithstanding any other provision of law, no person shall be subject to a penalty for failing to comply with a collection of information if it does not display a currently valid OMB control number.</td></tr>
</table>

| 1. REPORT DATE **AUG 2000** | 2. REPORT TYPE | 3. DATES COVERED **-** | |
|---|---|---|---|
| 4. TITLE AND SUBTITLE **Naval War College Style Manual and Classification Guide** | | 5a. CONTRACT NUMBER | |
| | | 5b. GRANT NUMBER | |
| | | 5c. PROGRAM ELEMENT NUMBER | |
| 6. AUTHOR(S) | | 5d. PROJECT NUMBER | |
| | | 5e. TASK NUMBER | |
| | | 5f. WORK UNIT NUMBER | |
| 7. PERFORMING ORGANIZATION NAME(S) AND ADDRESS(ES) **Naval War College,Newport ,RI,02841** | | 8. PERFORMING ORGANIZATION REPORT NUMBER | |
| 9. SPONSORING/MONITORING AGENCY NAME(S) AND ADDRESS(ES) | | 10. SPONSOR/MONITOR'S ACRONYM(S) | |
| | | 11. SPONSOR/MONITOR'S REPORT NUMBER(S) | |
| 12. DISTRIBUTION/AVAILABILITY STATEMENT **Approved for public release; distribution unlimited** | | | |
| 13. SUPPLEMENTARY NOTES **The original document contains color images.** | | | |
| 14. ABSTRACT **see report** | | | |
| 15. SUBJECT TERMS | | | |

| 16. SECURITY CLASSIFICATION OF: | | | 17. LIMITATION OF ABSTRACT | 18. NUMBER OF PAGES **78** | 19a. NAME OF RESPONSIBLE PERSON |
|---|---|---|---|---|---|
| a. REPORT **unclassified** | b. ABSTRACT **unclassified** | c. THIS PAGE **unclassified** | | | |

**Standard Form 298 (Rev. 8-98)**
Prescribed by ANSI Std Z39-18

Body-2

# U.S. Naval War College
## Style Manual and Classification Guide
### FOREWORD

This Style Manual and Classification Guide provides writers with information on development of papers or reports resulting from research or analytical efforts. It describes format and documentation and gives examples for the preparation of written documents.

Especially useful are the sections devoted to specific forms for footnote and bibliographic entries, pages 13 to 32. Formats included in those pages are generally consistent with the "Turabian"[1] system of citation. While several methods of citation are in general use today, Turabian provides a recognized standard system that is easy to use and universally understood. The examples in this publication will suffice for virtually all of the types of citations writers will need. In the rare instance that situations not covered here are encountered, multiple copies of Turabian are available in the Library.

This manual is complemented directly by the Naval War College Writing Guide, and by the Naval War College Library and its staff. The Writing Guide offers guidance and suggestions for conducting research and composing papers to satisfy curriculum requirements.

The Naval War College Library consists of extensive collections of books, documents, and other research materials, and a highly qualified staff to assist students and faculty in the use of these collections for study and research. The War College publication Research in the Library offers a useful starting point. For verification of factual data, suggestions for beginning or extending research, or locating materials, reference librarians are available to provide expert assistance. In this way valuable research time can be conserved.

For those papers or reports that require security classification, guidance is provided on determining classification and on obtaining authorization for classification. Sections pertinent to the classification process are extracted from the Department of the Navy Information Security Program Regulation. Instructions and samples are provided for depositing research papers in the Defense Technical Information Center.

---

[1] Named for Kate L. Turabian's A Manual for Writers of Term Papers, Theses, and Dissertations, 6th ed., rev. by John Grossman and Alice Bennett. (Chicago: The University of Chicago Press, 1996).

# STYLE MANUAL AND CLASSIFICATION GUIDE
## TABLE OF CONTENTS

# CHAPTER I

## FORMAT OF A RESEARCH PAPER

A Naval War College research paper should be scholarly. Reflecting the results of the author's individual research and analysis, it should be well documented and clearly written. Papers should be suitable for publication in a professional journal, such as the <u>Naval War College Review</u>, <u>Military Review</u>, <u>Air University Review</u>, <u>Parameters</u>, <u>Joint Force Quarterly</u>, or <u>Strategic Review</u>. Papers generally are organized in three sections: preliminaries, text, and reference materials.

### Preliminaries

Each element of the preliminaries begins on a separate page, and each page is designated in sequence by a lowercase Roman numeral.

<u>Title Page</u>. The title page is the first preliminary page of the paper. It is considered "page i," but is not numbered. The title page is prepared in the same manner as the samples in Appendix A.

<u>Abstract</u>. An abstract is a concise summary of the paper. It rarely exceeds one double-spaced typewritten page in length.[2] The primary objective of the abstract is to present the reader with the essentials of the paper in a highly condensed form.

An abstract is merely an abbreviated version of the paper. The author should attempt to capture the paper's purpose, its scope, and its findings and recommendations in the abstract. Because potential readers rely heavily on abstracts to help them cull from a large menu those papers that they will read in their entirety, abstracts tend to be marketing devices. This is not to say that the abstract should in any way incorrectly or unfairly represent the paper, but that it should be very carefully crafted.

When the authors prepare an abstract of their papers, the point of view should be the same as that of the paper. Accordingly, the tone and the approach of the abstract and the paper should be identical. This means that the abstract does not say: "The paper deals at length with the fatal voyage of the Russian fleet from its home waters in Europe to the Battle of Tsushima." Rather, it might say: "That the Russian naval squadron under Admiral Rozhdestvensky was soundly defeated at Tsushima by the Japanese fleet under Admiral Togo is of less interest than a study of the logistic demands of that fateful 18,000 mile journey."

<u>Preface</u>. Include an optional preface only to address matters that cannot properly be incorporated into the paper's Introduction. The author may wish to elaborate on reasons for

---

[2] A useful reference work on abstracts is: Harold Borko and Charles L. Bernier, <u>Abstracting Concepts and Methods</u> (New York: Academic Press, 1975).

1

embarking on the topic at hand, or to describe methods of research (e.g., questionnaires, interview techniques, sources of literature). In addition, the preface acknowledges, when applicable, special research assistance from persons and institutions. Ordinarily, the advice a student receives from a research advisor is not acknowledged.

Table of Contents. A table of contents is also optional. It lists the parts of the paper and their corresponding pagination. It provides the reader with a summary of the scope and the order of development of the author's argument.

List of Tables. If three or more tables are incorporated in the text, they should be indicated in a list of tables. For each table, the number of the table, its title, and corresponding pagination are given. Tables are numbered consecutively with capital Roman numerals.

List of Illustrations. If three or more maps, charts, graphs, or illustrations are used in the paper, provide a list of illustrations. List each entry as "Figure 1" or "Figure $n$" using Arabic instead of Roman numerals.

## Text

The text of the paper follows the preliminaries; each page is numbered in sequence with Arabic numerals. No specific format is prescribed for the text of the paper. Authors should be sensitive, however, to the presentation of their material. The flow should be logical and clear. Subheadings can be helpful to guide the reader. Conclusions and recommendations, as appropriate, should appear at the end of the paper. Authors frequently use the final parts of a paper to indicate additional problems or issues uncovered as a result of their effort, and to indicate potential fertile areas for further research. At the same time, authors should exercise care not to introduce new factual or analytical evidence in the conclusions section, and they should ensure that the conclusions follow from the evidence presented.

## Reference Materials

Reference materials for research papers include notes and a bibliography, and may embody an appendix or appendices, where applicable.

Notes. Notes are used to identify the source of significant information presented in the text. Notes may be presented either as footnotes at the bottom of text pages or as endnotes. Detailed instructions are contained in Chapter III.

Bibliography. The bibliography should contain entries of all sources used in the preparation of the paper including, in addition to all cited references, works consulted. It follows immediately after the endnotes.

Appendices. The appendix is employed to present relevant material not essential to the basic text. Examples include information of an unusually technical and complex nature;

2

discussion of methodology used in preparation of the paper, with sample questionnaires and a description of other data collection techniques presented; case studies too lengthy to be incorporated in the text; and documents not generally available to the reader. The appendix supplements the text, and authors must avoid the inclusion of data unrelated to the text.

Appendices may be numbered with Roman numerals or assigned letters to identify them. Page numbering may be sequential with the text, or a letter-number system may be adopted.

3

## CHAPTER II

PREPARING A PAPER

General Instructions

    Papers must be typed or prepared on a word processor and printed. The original must be submitted on 8 ½" x 11" white bond. Dark, clear printing is the standard. Dot matrix printers may not reproduce readable copy. Each department will issue instructions on the procedure for submission and binding of papers as well as on the submission of copies.

    Upon completion of the faculty evaluation, the paper, if unclassified, will be returned to the student with reviewers' remarks. Disposition of classified papers is provided for in Naval War College Standard Organization and Regulations Manual.

Stylistic Format

Margins.

| | |
|---|---|
| Top | 1" |
| Left | 1 - ¼" |
| Right | 1" |
| Bottom | 1" |

    Word Processing Fonts: Serif fonts are preferable to sans-serif fonts because the former are easier to read in blocks of text. This is an example of a serif font (Times New Roman). **This is an example of a sans-serif font (Arial).** Sans-serif fonts are better than serif fonts for display purposes (like signs), but are inferior to them for text.

    Line Spacing. Typing should be double-spaced throughout the paper, except that it should be single-spaced for footnotes, quotations over 50 words, the table of contents, and the bibliography. Appendices may be single-spaced.

    Page numbering. Pages are numbered in the center of each page, about one inch from the bottom edge of the paper. The pages of preliminary material (abstract, preface, table of contents, list of tables, list of illustrations) should be numbered with lowercase Roman numerals (ii, iii, iv, v). The title page is introductory page "i", but should not be numbered.

    Numbers. In general, use a figure for a number of 10 or more, unless it is the first word of a sentence. Numbers under 10 are spelled out, except for units of measurement, time, or money, which are always expressed in figures: e.g., 24 horses, $7, five homes, 4 hours. Similar rules apply to ordinal numbers, e.g. the fourth group, but the 10th lesson. Whenever

4

necessary for clarity, this rule can be dispensed with, i.e., when several numbers are compared as a group, they should all be written as numerals.

Spell out numbers related to dignified subjects: "the Ninety-ninth Congress."

Spell out indefinite expressions or round numbers: "the early seventies," "a thousand men," "one hundred-odd airplanes."

Spell out fractions standing alone: "one-half inch," "five one-thousandths."

Percentages. For percentages under 10, both the number and word "percent" are spelled out. Percentages of 10 or more, except at the beginning of a sentence, are written as figures: e.g., 12%.

Subnumbers and Subletters. Subnumbers and subletters are placed a half-line space below the line of writing: $H_2O$.

Superior Numbers and Superior Letters. Superior numbers and superior letters are placed a half-line space above the line of writing, for example, in the case of a footnote: as stated by Senator Fulbright.[2] Many word processors will automatically reduce the size of the superior letters or numbers in order to maintain line spacing. Because the paper's text is double-spaced, the size of the superscripted character should not pose problems.

Alignment of Numerals. When numerals are aligned in tabular or outline form, the right-hand margin is aligned. This holds true whether the numerals are Arabic or Roman.

| | |
|---|---|
| 1 | I |
| 12 | II |
| 123 | III |

Underscoring. In a typewritten paper, underscoring is used to indicate material which would be in italics if the paper were in printed form. If word processors permit the use of italics, they are acceptable instead of underlining. Do not, however, mix underlining and italics. The purpose of underscoring or italicizing is to emphasize letters, words, or phrases so that the thought they convey can be quickly comprehended; to indicate foreign words appearing in English text unless the words have been adopted into the English language; or to designate titles of books, full-length plays, pamphlets, magazines, newspapers, and journals. Parts of books and magazines--chapters, articles--are set off by quotation marks. For example: A. Lawrence Lowell's essay "Democracy and the Constitution" appears in Essays on Government. The initial letters of all-important words are capitalized in articles, as they are in book titles.

5

Names of Ships. The first reference to the name of a ship is formal, e.g. the U.S.S. Topeka (CLG-8). All subsequent reference should use an abbreviated (underlined) form: the Topeka, or just Topeka.

Conventions for Use within Quotations. In using quoted material, certain rules must be observed.

Omissions (Ellipsis). Omissions of sentences or parts of sentences may be made only if they do not destroy or distort the author's meaning. The omission should be indicated by the use of ellipses marks (three spaced periods . . .). When they appear at the end of a sentence, the ellipses marks should be followed by a period or other appropriate end-mark of punctuation, e.g., "our only test . . . is what is actually desired. . . ." The use of ellipsis should be sparing, and care must be taken not to distort either the context or the meaning of the foreshortened citation.

Additions (Brackets). Brackets are used to insert immediate editorial comment--to supply an essential date, name, or explanation, for example. Because brackets disturb the original quotation, they should be used infrequently. They are to be clearly distinguished from parentheses, which are used in quoted material only as they appear in the original.

Sic. Sic, meaning "thus," is used within brackets and underlined immediately following an apparent error, misspelling, or questionable assertion in the quoted material, or when the author wishes to insist upon the literal accuracy of the form in which a statement or word appears: e.g., "the forth [sic] of July."

Placement of the Quotation Marks. When quotation marks enclose dialogue the closing punctuation always goes inside the marks. For example, Fred called to his friend: "Tom, hurry back!"

When they are used in text that does not convey speech, commas and periods go inside the quotation marks, but semicolons and colons always go outside. Question marks and exclamation points depend on whether they apply to the entire sentence or just the quoted part: e.g., Why did she say, "Shut up," I wonder?

Verse Quotations. These should be typed in verse form, the line arrangement and indentions following those in the original work. Verse quotations are indented both left and right, and centered as nearly as possible. Single-spaced indented matter is not enclosed in quotation marks.

Hyphen and Dash. In typed material, a hyphen and a dash are made differently. A hyphen consists of one mark (-): e.g., "the man-eating shark." A dash consists of two marks not separated by space from the text (--): e.g., "these are shore deposits--gravel, sand, and

6

clay--but marine deposits underlie them." Word processors often employ <u>en</u>-dashes and <u>em</u>-dashes to indicate hyphens and dashes, respectively.

    <u>Division of Words</u>. A common use of the hyphen or <u>en</u>-dash is to indicate the continuation of a word divided at the end of a line. However, certain rules for the division of words should be followed.

- The repeated division of words at the end of lines should be avoided so far as possible without sacrificing good spacing.

- Hyphenated words are preferably divided at the compounding hyphen.

- A word should not be divided on a single letter; division on two letters should be avoided if possible.

- The last word on a page is not normally divided.

- Such abbreviations as USMC, USN, DC, A.M., and acronyms should not be divided.

- Initials should not be separated from the names to which they belong.

- The dictionary should always be consulted when there is a question of proper syllabication.

    <u>Abbreviations</u>. Abbreviate with caution to avoid confusing the reader. Abbreviations not universally recognized should be placed in parentheses and preceded in the text by the spelled-out forms the <u>first</u> time they occur. If an abbreviation or acronym is not to be used standing alone later, it need not be introduced. In tables, explanatory matter should be supplied in a footnote.

    Abbreviations with periods appear without spacing, e.g. U.S., U.S.S.R., N.Y. Acronyms and initials for governmental agencies and other organized bodies are presented without periods (exception: U.N.): e.g., NATO, MIT, AFL-CIO. When used as an adjective, United States may be abbreviated, but not as a noun: e.g., U.S. foreign policy, U.S. Congress, the policy of the United States. Names of foreign countries, except the former U.S.S.R., are not abbreviated. Plural acronyms are written without an apostrophe: e.g. OCAs (own courses of action).

    <u>Tables</u>. The objective of a table is to communicate, in a clear and concise format, material that cannot be displayed as clearly in any other way. Tabular information should be kept as simple as possible so that the meaning of the data will be obvious to the reader. Normally, a table will appear on the same page as the text that describes it. Should there be insufficient space remaining on the page to accommodate the table, the page should be   com-

pleted with text and the table presented on the following page.  When using a series of tables that would interrupt the text, consider incorporating them in an appendix instead.

An extensive description of tabular work is presented in the United States Government Printing Office Style Manual (REF Z 253 U58 1984).

Illustrations.  Figures (e.g., charts, diagrams, graphs, maps, or photographs) offer other ways to present information in visual form.  The three most common types of illustrations used in reporting research are the line chart, bar graph, and area chart.  Some types of charts are more effective than others to display particular types of data.  Most manuals for chart-making software provide guidelines on the preferred types of figure to display particular types of data.

Figures are numbered, in Arabic numerals, above the illustration.  Each figure will have a title, which appears beneath the figure number.

8

## CHAPTER III

### NOTES AND BIBLIOGRAPHY

An author acknowledges the source of reference material used in the preparation of a paper by means of notes, footnotes, and bibliographic entries. Such documentation protects an author from being held responsible for the authenticity of another writer's research, and serves as a convenience to the reader using the paper. Documentation is important because neither plagiarism nor close paraphrasing is acceptable. The format for documentation is specified; no one is privileged to make up his or her own system of citation. The format helps ensure that all needed information on the location of the material is included.

A footnote is a supplementary statement that provides information at a specific point in the text, whereas the bibliography is a compilation of all the reference sources used for the paper. This chapter will examine both the similarities and peculiarities of each type of acknowledgment. It will also discuss the procedure for obtaining permission from the originator for the use of certain materials in a paper. In addition, there are included selective listings of publishers' names and other bibliographic terminology in acceptably abbreviated form.

### Notes and Footnotes

Types of Notes and Footnotes. The three most common types of footnotes are explanatory footnotes, cross-reference footnotes, and citation or documentary footnotes.

Explanatory footnotes are amplifications of the text that, if included in the body of the text, would interrupt the train of thought. They may be given with or without supporting references. Avoid heavy use of this device by omitting unnecessary supplementary material from the paper or seeking to accommodate the material smoothly into the text.

Cross-reference footnotes are used to refer the reader to other parts of the paper. They may be combined with references to other works or with explanatory remarks. To avoid unnecessary distractions to the reader, they should be used sparingly.

The citation or documentary note, which is by far the most common type, is used to identify the source of significant information found in the text. Significant information may appear as a direct or indirect quotation or as a statement of fact. In order for a quotation to require a documentary note, however, it must not be so familiar that it is "in the public domain": the quotation "Give me liberty or give me death!" would not ordinarily be cited. Similarly, the statement of a generally accepted or well-known fact, such as the observation that George Washington was the first president of the United States, is not noted. Authors are called upon to use good judgment, based upon a consideration of the context and the guidelines presented above, in determining which material should be noted. The general rule: "When in doubt, provide a citation," applies.

9

Placement, Form, and Numbering of Notes and Footnotes. Explanatory notes and cross-reference notes will be presented in the form of footnotes; that is, they are placed at the bottom of the page containing the material to which they refer. Citation or documentary notes will be arranged either as footnotes or as endnotes--a separate section immediately following the appendices of the paper, immediately preceding the bibliography.

Thus, there are two methods of notation. One can choose only footnotes, or footnotes and endnotes. In the former, all notes and citations appear at the bottom of the page and are sequentially numbered throughout the paper. This applies whether the notes are explanatory, cross-reference, citation/documentary, or tabular. In the latter method, explanatory and cross-reference footnotes are placed at the bottom of the page, marked by one or more asterisks. Citation or documentary footnotes are numbered sequentially throughout the paper, and appear at the end as NOTES. The choice of whether to use only footnotes or footnotes and endnotes is left to the author.

Place footnotes at the bottom of the page containing the material to which they refer. Separate them from the text by a line extending about 1-½ inches from the left margin. Single-space within notes, and double-space between them. The bottom margin and page number will continue to meet the specifications described for regular text.

For ENDNOTES, center the title NOTES[3] on the page, but title only the first page of endnotes. Double-space the first note below the title. Single-space individual notes, and double-space between them.

Because word processors differ in the manner in which they handle notes, two formats are possible. In the first, the number of the note is superscripted both for footnotes and end-notes. In the second, the number is not superscripted, and it is followed by a period and two spaces. Either method is acceptable.

## Bibliography

Content of Bibliography. A bibliography is a compilation of writings related to and consulted for the paper. A bibliography contains references to all basic written sources cited in the text of the paper and the footnotes, as well as all other written matter the author found helpful in preparing the paper. Only basic sources, not chapters or small parts thereof, are entered in a bibliography. Whether or not such ephemeral material as letters, interviews, and telephone conversations appears in the bibliography is left to the author's discretion.

Form of Entries. The first line of each bibliographic entry is flush with the left-hand margin and following lines are indented five spaces from the margin. Entries are single-spaced internally and separated by double-spacing.

---

[3] Turabian, 277 .

10

Bibliographic entries are listed alphabetically by the author's last name, or, if no author is given, by the first important word in the title. In second and succeeding entries for works by the same author, the name of the author is not given. Instead, the author's name is replaced by a line segment eight spaces long. For government documents each repeated unit of the author entry is replaced by such a line segment. If the entire author entries are the same for two or more works, they are arranged alphabetically by title.

Examples:

Grove, Eric. Battle for the Fjords: NATO's Forward Maritime Strategy in Action. Annapolis, MD: Naval Institute Press, 1991.

_____. Vanguard to Trident: British Naval Policy Since World War II. Annapolis, MD: Naval Institute Press, 1987.

Huntington, Samuel P. American Politics: The Promise of Disharmony. Cambridge, MA: Belknap Press, 1981.

_____. The Clash of Civilizations and the Remaking of World Order. New York: Simon & Schuster, 1996.

### Content of Bibliographic Entries and First-Reference Notes

Parts in Common. Aside from the obvious differences between bibliographic entries and first-reference notes (order of author's name, punctuation, and use of parentheses), the two types of acknowledgment are comparable in content. The items of information they both provide are discussed below.

Author. The author's name should include given name, family name, and middle initial(s). Titles such as doctor, professor, or captain, together with the author's position and degrees held, should be omitted; titles of nobility before given names or initials, however, should be included. If the work was issued by an organization without naming an author, the official title of the organization should be entered in place of the name of the author. If an editor, translator, or compiler is to be listed instead of an author, the name should be followed by a comma and "ed.," "trans.," or "comp."

Title. In a title, the first word and every word except articles, prepositions, and conjunctions should be capitalized. The title of a complete published work, such as a book or a series of books, is underlined. When a periodical article is acknowledged, the article title is placed in quotation marks and the periodical title is underlined. Titles of unpublished material, such as dissertations, are placed in quotation marks. Subtitles need not be included except when they are necessary to clarify the meaning or scope of the main title.

11

Edition. Editions of a work after the first shall be indicated by placing the appropriate abbreviation, such as "2d ed.," after the title.

Imprint. The imprint consists of the place of publication, name of publisher, and date of publication. The place of publication is indicated by the name of the city written out and the name of the state abbreviated using standard state abbreviations. For example, either "N.Y." or "NY" might be used, but states must be abbreviated consistently. The name of the state is omitted if the city is well known, or if the publisher is a state university press. If two or more cities appear under the publisher's imprint, only the first is listed. The abbreviation "n.p." is used if no place of publication is indicated.

The name of the publisher should be carefully and accurately transcribed. A list of commonly used shortened forms is given on page 33, but the rule "when in doubt use the form that appears on the publication's title page" should be adopted. When listing a publisher with subsidiary divisions, always list the major activity first, followed by the secondary division; for example:

> Georgetown University. Center for Strategic and International Studies
>
> Princeton University. Center for International Studies
>
> U.S. Air University. Air War College
>
> U.S. Dept. of the Army. Office of Military History

If the publisher is unknown, the abbreviation "n.p." should be used. When both place of publication and publisher are unknown, use "n.p.: n.p." If the publisher and the author are the same organization, the name of the publisher is omitted.

The date of publication is usually shown on the title page. If no data appears there, use the latest copyright date given on the back of the title page. The day, month, and year should appear if that information is provided. The abbreviation "n.d." shall be used if no date is given.

In notes, the exact location of the citation is shown by the page number, which follows the date of publication. The abbreviations "p" and "pp" (for "page" and "inclusive pages") are omitted except when confusion might occur. In the bibliography the inclusive pages of articles are usually provided.

Above all, be consistent. Use the same format throughout.

Examples. Turabian's A Manual for Writers of Term Papers, Theses, and Dissertations (REF LB 2369 T8 1996) contains many pages of examples of bibliographic and notation

12

entries. The examples provided herein are consistent with Turabian. The book itself should be consulted for situations not covered.

## BOOKS

<u>Single Author</u>

N       [1] Donald Kagan, <u>On the Origins of War and the Preservation of Peace</u> (New York: Doubleday 1995), 44.

B       Kagan, Donald. <u>On the Origins of War and the Preservation of Peace</u>. New York: Doubleday, 1995.


<u>No Author Given</u>

N       [2] <u>Harmonizing the Evolution of U.S. and Russian Defense Policies</u> (Washington, DC: CSIS, 1993), 77-78.

B       <u>Harmonizing the Evolution of U.S. and Russian Defense Policies</u>. Washington, DC: CSIS, 1993.


<u>Two (or Three) Authors</u>

N       [1] Alvin Toffler and Heidi Toffler, <u>War and Anti-War</u> (Boston: Little, Brown, 1993), 247.

B       Toffler, Alvin and Heidi Toffler. <u>War and Anti-War</u>. Boston: Little, Brown, 1993.


<u>More than Three Authors, One Volume</u>

N       [4] Marvin Gettleman and others, <u>El Salvador: Central America in the New Cold War</u> (New York: Grove Press, 1981), 339-341.

B       Gettleman, Marvin, Frederick Oursman, Louis Hirschhorn, and Donna B. Little. <u>El Salvador: Central America in the New Cold War</u>. New York: Grove Press, 1981.

13

## Titled Volume in Titled Series

N     [5] Winston S. Churchill and Franklin D. Roosevelt, <u>Churchill & Roosevelt: The Complete Correspondence, Vol. I, Alliance Emerging, October 1933-November 1942</u> (Princeton, NJ: Princeton University Press, 1984), 150-151.

B     Churchill, Winston S. and Franklin D. Roosevelt. <u>Churchill & Roosevelt: The Complete Correspondence. Vol. I, Alliance Emerging, October 1933-November 1942.</u> Princeton, NJ: Princeton University Press, 1984.

## Double Source

N     [1] Alan Dowty, <u>Middle East Crisis: U.S. Decision-Making in 1958, 1970, and 1973</u> (Berkeley: University of California Press, 1984), 143; Henry A. Kissinger, <u>The White House Years</u> (Boston: Little, Brown, 1979), 606.

B     Dowty, Alan. <u>Middle East Crisis: U.S. Decision-Making in 1958, 1970, and 1973.</u> Berkeley: University of California Press, 1984.

B     Kissinger, Henry A. <u>The White House Years</u>. Boston: Little, Brown, 1979.

## Edited Collection

N     [1] Jorge Heine, ed., <u>Time for Decision: The United States and Puerto Rico</u> (Lanham, MD: North-South, 1983), 154.

B     Heine, Jorge, ed. <u>Time for Decision: The United States and Puerto Rico</u>. Lanham, MD: North-South, 1983.

## Edition after the First

N     [1] Frederick H. Hartmann, <u>The Relations of Nations</u>, 6th ed. (New York: Macmillan, 1983), 125.

B     Hartmann, Frederick H. <u>The Relations of Nations</u>, 6th ed. New York: Macmillan, 1983.

14

## Quoted at Second Hand

N   [19] Wendell Willkie, quoted in Nigel Hamilton, <u>Master of the Battlefield: Monty's War Years, 1942-1944</u> (New York: McGraw-Hill, 1983), 4.

B   Hamilton, Nigel. <u>Master of the Battlefield: Monty's War Years, 1942-1944</u>. New York: McGraw-Hill, 1983.

N   [24] Louis Dufours, "The End of the Troubled Times," <u>Strategic Review</u> (Winter 1989): 71; quoted in Thomas Travers, <u>The Future of the Nation State</u> (Chicago: University of Chicago Press, 1993), 223.

B   Dufours, Louis. "The End of the Troubled Times." <u>Strategic Review</u>, Winter 1989, 71. Quoted in Thomas Travers, <u>The Future of the Nation State</u>, 223. Chicago: University of Chicago Press, 1993.

## Reprinted Work

N   [14] Trevor N. Dupuy, <u>A Genius for War</u> (Englewood Cliffs, NJ: Prentice-Hall, 1977; reprint, Fairfax, VA: Hero Books, 1984), 102 (page citation is to the reprint edition).

B   Dupuy, Trevor N. <u>A Genius for War</u>. Englewood Cliffs, NJ: Prentice-Hall, 1977. Reprint, Fairfax, VA: Hero Books, 1984.

## The Bible

N   [12] I Corinthians 13:10-13 NEB (New English Bible).

B   According to Turabian: "Well-known reference books are generally not listed in bibliographies." [See Turabian, p. 204]

## Publishing Organization as Author

N   [12] U.S. Congressional Budget Office, <u>Manpower for a 600-Ship Navy: Costs and Policy Alternatives</u> (Washington, DC: 1983), 10.

B   U.S. Congressional Budget Office. <u>Manpower for a 600-Ship Navy: Costs and Policy Alternatives</u>. Washington, DC: 1983.

## Published Report

15

N       [13] Inter-American Development Bank, <u>Annual Report, 1984</u> (Washington, DC: 1984), 60-61.

B       Inter-American Development Bank. <u>Annual Report, 1984</u>. Washington, DC: 1984.


## Paper in Series

N       [14] David Buchan, <u>Western Security and Economic Strategy towards the East</u>, Adelphi Papers, no. 192 (London: International Institute for Strategic Studies, 1984), 15.

B       Buchan, David. <u>Western Security and Economic Strategy towards the East</u>. Adelphi Papers, no. 192. London: International Institute for Strategic Studies, 1984.


## ARTICLES

### Periodical Article

N       [1] Pauline H. Baker, "South Africa on the Move," <u>Current History</u>, 14 (May 1990): 199.

B       Baker, Pauline H. "South Africa on the Move." <u>Current History</u>, 14 (May 1990): 197-200.


N       [2] "Will North Africa Be Next Hot Spot for U.S.?" <u>U.S. News & World Report</u>, 12 (March 1984): 35.

B       "Will North Africa Be Next Hot Spot for U.S.?" <u>U.S. News & World Report</u>, 12 (March 1984): 35-37.


N       [3] John L. Piotrowski, "The Challenge in Space: A Joint Effort," <u>U.S. Naval Institute Proceedings</u> (February 1990): 35.

B       Piotrowski, John L. "The Challenge in Space: A Joint Effort." <u>U.S. Naval Institute Proceedings</u> (February 1990): 32-36.

16

## Newspaper Article

N      4 Richard Harwood and Haynes Johnson, "The War's Final Battle," <u>Washington Post</u>, 14 April 1985, sec. 1, p. 2.

B      Newspapers are not usually listed in the bibliography.

N      [5] Drew Middleton. "Persian Gulf War: Iranian Offensive Delayed," <u>New York Times</u>, 6 April 1984, 9:2.

B      Newspapers are not usually listed in the bibliography.

## Article in Foreign Language Journal

N      [6] Benoît Bouchet, "La Qualité et les Armées," <u>Défense Nationale</u>, avril 1990, 77.

B      Bouchet, Benoît. "La Qualité et les Armées." <u>Défense Nationale</u>, avril 1990, 71-87.

## English Translation of Soviet Periodical

N      [7] D.F. Ustinov, "Ustinov Stresses Soviet Military Strength--and Says U.S. Is Increasing Danger of War," <u>The Current Digest of the Soviet Press</u>, 21 March 1984, 10. Translated from <u>Pravda</u>, 23 February 1984.

B      Ustinov, D.F. "Ustinov Stresses Soviet Military Strength-and Says U.S. Is Increasing Danger of War." <u>The Current Digest of the Soviet Press</u>, 21 March 1984, 10-11. Translated from <u>Pravda</u>, 23 February 1984.

## Translation of Article--JPRS Entry

N      [8] V. Tomin, "The NATO Exercise 'Ocean Safari-83'," U.S. Joint Publications Research Service, <u>USSR Report: Military Affairs</u>, JPRS-UMA-84-031 (Washington, DC: JPRS, 11 April 1984), 65.

B      Tomin, V. "The NATO Exercise 'Ocean Safari-83'." <u>USSR Report: Military Affairs</u>. JPRS-UMA-84-031. Washington, DC: JPRS, 11 April 1984, 64-68.

17

## Encyclopedia Article

N    [9]   The New Encyclopaedia Britannica, Micropaedia, 15th ed., s.v. "Vietnam war."

B    According to Turabian: "Well-known reference books are generally not listed in bibliographies." [See Turabian, p. 204]


## Article in Edited Collection

N    [11]   Joseph G. Brennan, "The Stockdale Course," in Teaching Values and Ethics in College, ed. Michael J. Collins (San Francisco: Jossey-Bass, 1983), 72.

B    Brennan, Joseph G. "The Stockdale Course." In Teaching Values and Ethics in College, edited by Michael J. Collins, 60-81. San Francisco: Jossey-Bass, 1983.


## Article in Serial Publication

N    [12]   "East Germany--Disintegration of Communist-Led Government--Round Table Talks," Keesing's Record of World Events, January 1990, 37171.

B    "East Germany--Disintegration of Communist-Led Government--Round Table Talks." Keesing's Record of World Events, January 1990, 37170-37172.


N    [14]   R. P. Largess, "Reviving the Naval Airship," Naval Forces, no. 1 (1990): 13.

B    Largess, R. P. "Reviving the Naval Airship." Naval Forces, no. 1 (1990): 12-14.

18

## CD-ROM

Compact Disc, Read-Only Memory (CD-ROM) has become commonplace in libraries as an efficient way to make research data widely available. At the NWC Library, CD-ROM tools fall into one of two categories: periodical and document indexes, and full-text sources. Both types normally allow the user to access the entire database by keyword searching, as well as by more pinpointed field searching. Another useful feature of these tools is the capability to print or download search results. The following examples are from CD-ROM databases used at the Library.

Citations of full-text documents from CD-ROM databases should include the following data elements, where applicable and available:

- the author's name

- the title of article, in quotation marks

- the date of publication, or last revision

- the title of the CD-ROM, underlined

- the place of publication, publisher, and the date of publication

Example:

N    [16] James J. Tritten, "Naval Perspectives for Military Doctrine Development," 23 October 1995, Joint Electronic Library CD-ROM, Washington, DC: Joint Chiefs of Staff, April 1996.

B    Tritten, James J. "Naval Perspectives for Military Doctrine Development." 23 October 1995. Joint Electronic Library CD-ROM. Washington, DC: Joint Chiefs of Staff, April 1996.

N    [17] "France, Defense Organization/Strength, Organization/Order of Battle," 1 July 1995, <Nations/NATO/France/Defense Organization/Strength/Overview> U.S. Naval Institute Periscope Database, Rockville, MD: United Communications Group, April 1996.

B    "France, Defense Organization/Strength, Organization/Order of Battle." 1 July 1995. <Nations/NATO/France/Defense Organization/Strength/Overview> U.S. Naval Institute Periscope Database. Rockville, MD: United Communications Group, April 1996.

19

## U.S. GOVERNMENT DOCUMENTS

Congressional Committee

N      [1] Congress, Senate, Committee on Armed Services, <u>Defense Organization: the Need for Change</u>, Staff Report, 99th Cong., 1st sess. (Washington, DC: GPO, 1985), 521-522.

B      U.S. Congress. Senate. Committee on Armed Services. <u>Defense Organization: the Need for Change</u>. Staff Report. 99th Cong., 1st sess. Washington, DC: GPO, 1985.

N      [2] Congress, House, Committee on Appropriations, <u>Department of Defense Appropriations for 1985: Hearing before the Committee on Appropriations</u>, 99th Cong., 1st sess., 14 February 1985, pt. 8, 132-150.

B      U.S. Congress. House. Committee on Appropriations. <u>Department of Defense Appropriations for 1985: Hearing before the Committee on Appropriations</u>, 99th Cong., 1st sess., 14 February 1985.

Congressional Committee: Subcommittee

N      [3] Congress, Senate, Committee on Appropriations, <u>El Salvador Military and Economic Reprogramming: Hearing before the Subcommittee on Foreign Relations Appropriations</u>, 98th Cong, 1st sess., 6 June 1983, 77.

B      U.S. Congress. Senate. Committee on Appropriations. <u>El Salvador Military and Economic Reprogramming: Hearing before the Subcommittee on Foreign Relations Appropriations</u>. 98th Cong, 1st sess., 6 June 1983.

Joint Committee

N      [5] Congress, Joint Economic Committee, <u>1985 Economic Report of the President: Hearing before the Joint Economic Committee</u>, 98th Cong, 2d sess., 22 March 1984, 117.

B      U.S. Congress. Joint Economic Committee. <u>1985 Economic Report of the President: Hearing before the Joint Economic Committee</u>. 98th Cong, 2d sess, 22 March 1984.

20

## Testimony of Individuals

N      [6] John B. Breaux, "Statement," U.S. Congress, House, Committee on Foreign Affairs, U.S. Foreign Policy and the Law of the Sea, Hearings before the Committee on Foreign Affairs, 97th Cong, 2d sess., 6 April 1982, 9-22.

B      U.S. Congress. House. Committee on Foreign Affairs. U.S. Foreign Policy and the Law of the Sea: Hearings before the Committee on Foreign Affairs. 97th Cong, 2d sess., 6 April 1982.

## Department of Defense Agencies

N      [1] Joint Deployment Agency, Joint Deployment System Functional Description (MacDill Air Force Base, FL: 1985), 24.

B      U.S. Joint Deployment Agency. Joint Deployment System Functional Description. MacDill Air Force Base, FL: 1985.

## Instruction

N      [2] Navy Department, Navy Tactical Development and Evaluation and Fleet Mission Program Library, OPNAVINST 5401.6J (Washington, DC: 1990), 7.

B      U.S. Navy Department. Navy Tactical Development and Evaluation and Fleet Mission Program Library. OPNAVINST 5401.6J. Washington, DC: 1990.

## Report

N      [3] Department of Defense, Report on Allied Contributions to the Common Defense (Washington, DC: 1983), 39-48.

B      U.S. Department of Defense. Report on Allied Contributions to the Common Defense. Washington, DC: 1983.

21

## Doctrinal Publications

N    [1] Joint Chiefs of Staff, <u>Joint Doctrine for Command and Control Warfare</u>, Joint Pub 3-13.1 (Washington, DC: 7 February 1996), II-8.

B    U.S. Joint Chiefs of Staff.  <u>Joint Doctrine for Command and Control Warfare.</u>  Joint Pub 3-13.1. Washington, DC: 7 February 1996.


## Non-Department of Defense Agencies

N    [6] General Accounting Office, <u>Logistics Support Costs for the B-1B Aircraft Can Be Reduced</u>, <u>Report to the Secretary of Defense</u> (Washington, DC:  1984), 32.

B    U.S. General Accounting Office. <u>Logistics Support Costs for the B-1B Aircraft Can Be Reduced</u>.  Report to the Secretary of Defense. Washington, DC:  1984.


N    [26] Central Intelligence Agency, Directorate of Intelligence, <u>Appearances of Soviet Leaders January-December 1986</u> (Washington, DC:  1987), 95-98.

B    U.S. Central Intelligence Agency.  Directorate of Intelligence.  <u>Appearances of Soviet Leaders January - December 1986</u>.  Washington, DC:  1987.


## Contractors

N    [3.] Center for Naval Analyses, Naval Studies Group,  <u>Retention and Career Force Quality</u>, CRC 518 (Alexandria, VA:  1984), 7.

B    Center for Naval Analyses.  Naval Studies Group.  <u>Retention and Career Force Quality</u>. CRC 518.  Alexandria, VA:  1984.


N    [4] Bruce Hoffman, <u>More than Meets the Eye:  The Seizure of the Achille Lauro</u>, P-7147, (Santa Monica, CA:  Rand, 1985), 2.

B    Hoffman, Bruce. <u>More than Meets the Eye:  The Seizure of the Achille Lauro</u>. P-7147. Santa Monica, CA:  Rand, 1985.

22

## U.S. Laws, Treaties, Regulations

Code of Federal Regulations

N     [1] "United States Navy Regulations and Official Records," Code of Federal Regulations, Title 32--National Defense (Washington, DC: U.S. General Services Administration, National Archives and Records Service, Office of the Federal Register, 1 July 1983), chap. VI, 700-701.

B     Code of Federal Regulations, Title 32--National Defense. Washington, DC: U.S. General Services Administration. National Archives and Records Service. Office of the Federal Register, 1 July 1983.

Executive Order

N     [2] President, Executive Order, "Manual for Courts Martial, United States, 1984," Federal Register 49, no. 2 (23 April 1984), 17358.

B     U.S. President. Executive Order. "Manual for Courts Martial, United States, 1984." Federal Register 49, no. 2 (23 April 1984): 17152-17430.

Presidential Proclamation

N     [4] President, Proclamation, "Death of Federal Diplomatic and Military Personnel in Beirut, Lebanon," Weekly Compilation of Presidential Documents (25 April 1983), 571.

B     U.S. President. Proclamation. "Death of Federal Diplomatic and Military Personnel in Beirut, Lebanon." Weekly Compilation of Presidential Documents (25 April 1983): 571.

U.S. Code

N     [15] General Military Law, U.S. Code, Title 10, secs. 101-2801 (1992).

B     General Military Law. U.S. Code, Title 10, secs. 101-2801 (1992).

Treaty

23

N    [22] Department of State, "Safety of Life at Sea," 22 January 1995, <u>United States Treaties and Other International Agreements</u>, TIAS no. 9700 vol. 32, pt. 1, 47-292.

B    U.S. Department of State. "Safety of Life at Sea," 22 January 1995. <u>United States Treaties and Other International Agreements</u>, TIAS no. 9700. vol. 32, pt. 1.


<u>U.S. Government Documents--Periodicals</u>

N    [7] Congress, House, "Condemning the Assassination of U.S. Naval Attache in Athens," <u>Congressional Record</u> 129, no. 133, (17 November 1983): 16466.

B    U.S. Congress. House. "Condemning the Assassination of U.S. Naval Attaché in Athens." Congressional Record 129, no. 133, (17 November 1983).


## International Organization Documents

<u>United Nations</u>

N    [1] Hague, International Court of Justice, <u>Fisheries Jurisdiction Cases</u> ([The Hague]: 1975), v. 1, 27-38.

B    Hague. International Court of Justice. <u>Fisheries Jurisdiction Cases</u>. [The Hague]: 1975, 2v.


N    [2] United Nations, Economic and Social Council, <u>Official Records: Population Commission</u>, 22d sess., supplement No. 2, E/1984/12; E/CN. 9/1984/9 (New York: 1984), 24.

B    United Nations. Economic and Social Council. <u>Official Records: Population Commission</u>. 22d sess., supplement No. 2. E/1984/12; E/CN. 9/1984/9. New York: 1984.


N    [13] United Nations Conference on the Law of the Sea, 3d, <u>United Nations Convention on the Law of the Sea</u>, A/CONF. 62/122 (n.p.: 1982), 12.

B    United Nations Conference on the Law of the Sea, 3d. <u>United Nations Convention on the Law of the Sea</u>. A/CONF. 62/122. n.p.: 1982.


24

## Other United Nations Agencies

N      [16] International Atomic Energy Agency, <u>Guidebook on the Introduction of Nuclear Power</u> (Vienna: 1982), 43.

B      International Atomic Energy Agency. <u>Guidebook on the Introduction of Nuclear Power</u>. Vienna: 1982.

<u>Other International Organizations</u>

<u>GATT</u>

N      [11] Contracting Parties to the General Agreement on Tariffs and Trade, <u>GATT Activities in 1983</u> (Geneva: 1984), 59.

B      Contracting Parties to the General Agreement on Tariffs and Trade. <u>GATT Activities in 1983</u>. Geneva: 1984.

<u>NATO</u>

N      [22] North Atlantic Treaty Organization, <u>NATO Handbook</u> (Brussels: NATO Information Service, 1989), 13-16.

B      North Atlantic Treaty Organization. <u>NATO Handbook</u>. Brussels: NATO Information Service, 1989.

<u>OAS</u>

N      [31] Organization of American States, Secretary General, <u>Annual Report of the Secretary General, 1980</u>, OEA/Ser. D/III. 31 (Washington, DC: 1980), 10-11.

B      Organization of American States. Secretary General. <u>Annual Report of the Secretary General, 1980</u>. OEA/Ser. D/III. 31. Washington, DC: 1980.

<u>OECD</u>

25

N        [32] Organisation for Economic Co-operation and Development, <u>Economic Surveys:</u> <u>Greece</u> (Paris: 1993), 50.

B        Organisation for Economic Co-operation and Development. <u>Economic Surveys:</u> <u>Greece</u>. Paris: 1993.

## ELECTRONIC DOCUMENTS

The author must use judgment when applying these suggested formats, allowing for the myriad of possibilities in linkage and access. The goal is to be clear, consistent, and allow the reader to find the cited sources in the easiest way possible.

Examples shown throughout are in citation format for a bibliography. To convert citations to note format, separate data elements with commas.

<u>World Wide Web (WWW) Sites</u>:

A specific document found on a Web page should include these data elements, if known, in this order:

- the author's name

- the full title of the document in quotation marks

- the title of the complete work, underlined

- the date of publication, or last revision

- the full http address (URL), in angle brackets

- the date of the visit to the Web page on which the information was collected, in square brackets.

<u>Example</u>:

"Daily List of Documents Issued at Headquarters." <u>United Nations Daily List of</u> <u>Documents</u>. 9 July 1996. <http://www.un.org/docs/dl/latest.htm/> [14 August 1997].

It is often helpful to indicate the context in which a particular Web page or document is found. The reader may wish to locate similar material posted at the same site; by displaying the context, the reader can be led to a group of related materials. Context can be described by using "linked" or "Lkd." Be sure to include:

- the author's name

26

- the full title of the document in quotation marks

- the date of publication, or last revision

- the abbreviation Lkd., meaning "linked from"

- linked site details

- the full http address (URL), in angle brackets

- the date of your visit to the Web page, in parentheses.

Example:

"Forward from the Sea." Lkd. U.S. Navy Vision Publications at "Service Vision Publications Page." http://www.dtic.mil:80/doctrine/jv2010/jvsvc.htm/> [23 July 1998].

E-Mail:

Citations for e-mail you personally receive should include:

- the author's name

- the author's e-mail address, in angle brackets

- the subject line from the e-mail, in quotation marks

- notation of recipient of E-mail, and recipient's address in square brackets.

- date of receipt.

Examples:

Thornton, Dave R. <d.r.thornton@durham.ac.uk> "LAN-CD." [E-mail to Julie Zecher <zecherj@nwc.navy.mil>] 11 July 1999.

Goncalo, Elizabeth. <goncaloe@nwc.navy.mil> "GPO Access Workshop." [E-mail to George Kasten <kasteng@hotmail.com>]1 June 2000.

Commercial Sources (LEXIS-NEXIS, for example):

Data elements to be included, in the following order, are:

- the author's name

27

- the title of the article, in quotation marks

- the title of the publication (journal, newspaper, wire service, etc.), underlined

- the date of publication

- the Library and File, separated by a slash, if applicable

- the name of the online service, underlined

- the place of publication, and publisher

- the date of access, in parentheses

Example:

Baum, Bob. "Americans Endure Long Distance Running Medal Drought." The
Associated Press. 22 July 1996. News/Wires. Lexis-Nexis. Dayton, OH:
Lexis-Nexis. (23 July 1996)

## Classified Documents

If it is necessary either to make reference to a classified document or to quote unclassified parts of a classified document, the citations in notes and bibliographies should not make reference to the fact that the document cited is classified. Thus, one should not put "(U)" after the title of the referenced publication, nor should one indicate the overall classification of the reference anywhere in a note or bibliographical entry. If the title is classified (some agencies do not affix separate title classifications), then it cannot be cited in an unclassified paper.

Citations of full-text files found on CD-ROMs in the Classified Library must include the security classification of the particular file, as well as the classification of the entire database. Data elements for citations from Classified CD-ROMs should include, in the following order:

1. the title of the Lesson Learned, in quotation marks

2. the Lesson Learned or JULLS number

3. the Update date

4. the security classification of the Lesson Learned

5. the title of the database, underlined

28

6. the title of the CD-ROM, underlined, preceded by "Available on"

7. the place of publication, publisher, and date of publication

8. the security classification of the CD-ROM.

Examples:

N       "Hurricane Bob Consolidated Lessons Learned for Hampton Roads VA Area," Lessons Learned No. LLEAO-03174, 30 January 1996. Unclassified. Navy Lessons Learned Database (NLLDB), Available on Navy Tactical Information Compendium (NTIC) CD-ROM Series. Washington, DC: Naval Tactical Support Activity, March 1996, SECRET/NF.

B  "Hurricane Bob Consolidated Lessons Learned for Hampton Roads VA Area." Lessons Learned No. LLEAO-03174. 30 January 1996. Unclassified. Navy Lessons Learned Database (NLLDB). Available on Navy Tactical Information Compendium (NTIC) CD-ROM Series A. Washington, DC: Naval Tactical Support Activity, March 1996. SECRET/NF.

See Chapter IV, SECURITY, for additional information on working with classified material.

29

**Unpublished Materials**

Letter

N        [33] Frederick D. Wolf to John F. Lehman, Jr., 12 October 1984, Navy Library, "Letters of John F. Lehman, Jr.," Navy Yard, Washington, DC

B        Wolf, Frederick D., to John F. Lehman, Jr. 12 October 1984. Navy Library. "Letters of John F. Lehman, Jr." Navy Yard. Washington, DC

Unpublished Thesis

N        [41] Anthony P. Tokarz, "Legal Implications for U.S. Marine Corps Deployments in Lebanon," (Unpublished Research Paper, U.S. Naval War College, Newport, RI: 1983), 5.

B        Tokarz, Anthony P. "Legal Implications for U.S. Marine Corps Deployments in Lebanon." Unpublished Research Paper, U.S. Naval War College, Newport, RI: 1983.

Interview: See section on "Special Permission," page 32.

N        [6] Dr. J.A. Knauss, Vice President for Marine Affairs, and Dean, Graduate School of Oceanography, University of Rhode Island, interview by author, 1 December 1996, tape recording, University of Rhode Island, Greeley Hall, Kingston, R.I.

B        Knauss, J.A., Vice President for Marine Affairs, and Dean, Graduate School of Oceanography, University of Rhode Island. Interview by author, 1 December 1996. Tape recording. University of Rhode Island, Greeley Hall, Kingston, R.I. .

Lecture: See section on "Special Permission," page 32.

N        [4] Alvin H. Bernstein, "Clausewitz in Context," Lecture, U.S. Naval War College, Newport, RI: 3 December 1983.

B        Bernstein, Alvin H. "Clausewitz in Context." Lecture. U.S. Naval War College, Newport, RI: 3 December 1983.

Telephone Conversation

N        [11] Fred C. Ikle, Under Secretary of Defense for Policy, telephone conversation with author, 2 April 1984.

B        Ikle, Fred C. Under Secretary of Defense for Policy. Telephone conversation with author, 2 April 1984.

30

## Subsequent Reference Notes

After the required information about a source has been furnished in a first-reference documentary note, it is not necessary to repeat all information in subsequent notes for that source. Subsequent reference notes must, however, clearly identify the source.

The Brief Form. Second and following references to a source are made by listing only the last name of the author(s) or editor(s), followed by the appropriate volume number (if any) and page reference, so long as they occur within the same chapter.

Examples:

[7] Faulkner, ed., v. IV, 17.

[9] Stillman and Pfaff, 62.

[13] Senate Appropriations Committee, 429.

If more than one work by the same author, editor, or organization has been previously cited, the title--or an abbreviation--of the referenced work must be included in each subsequent note.

Examples:

[15] Kennedy, Profiles, 127.

[18] Deutsch, Nationalism, 71.

Subsequent references to an article with no author given are made by using only the title for identification.

Example:

[21] "Twenty Hours at Bay," 10-12.

Use of Ibid. The use of the abbreviation ibid. (ibidem, Lat., "in the same place") is a common variation to the brief form of subsequent reference notes. When references to the same work follow each other without any intervening reference, ibid. is used in the new entry. If a different page number is needed in the new entry, it must follow ibid.

Examples:

[22] Hairston, 71.

[23] Ibid.

31

[24] Ibid., 75-78.

Since ibid. refers to place, it must not be used as a substitute for the author's name when references to two different works by the same author directly follow each other.

Examples:

[25] Mitchell, Advance, 70.

[26] Ibid., Logistics, 13. (Incorrect)

[27] Mitchell, Logistics, 13 (Correct)

Avoid a long list of Ibid. citations in the notes section by combining them. Furthermore, when a discussion in a particular segment of the paper is based on the research of another writer, an explanatory footnote may be used to so indicate, thereby eliminating the need for frequent and repetitious references.

## Special Permission

It is often necessary to obtain special permission from the originator of both classified and unclassified materials before they can be used in a paper. Since lectures and interviews are "privileged" material, special permission must always be obtained in writing from the lecturer or inter-viewee before such remarks may be quoted. The Naval War College's Nonattribution Policy is outlined in the Standard Organization and Regulations Manual.

Normal use of copyrighted materials in scholarly efforts, such as student papers, does not require special permission from the copyright authority. If the student is considering submitting a paper for publication, however, special permission will often be necessary. Moreover, students should obtain permission when quoting extensively from materials, or when incorporating these materials in their entirety into a paper. The student should be aware that copyrighted materials include such items as maps, photographs, drawings, and tables as well as text, and should exercise proper caution in reproduction and use. In the event that special permission to use copyrighted material is required, the student shall submit a request through the appropriate academic department to the Copyright/Editorial Division, containing the following information: title of source of material, name of author, name of publisher, date of publication, exact passage(s) required, and explanation and date of proposed use. About an eight weeks' period is generally required to obtain copyright clearance. Further information on the use of copyrighted materials is given in SECNAVINST 5870.l series.

32

## Selected List of Publishers

### (Shortened Form)

| | |
|---|---|
| ABC-Clio | Naval Institute Press |
| Aero | Naval War College Press |
| American Enterprise Institute | Nijhoff |
| Atheneum | Northwestern University Press |
| Ballinger | Norton |
| Basic | Oceana |
| Brookings Institution | Oxford University Press |
| Cambridge University Press | Pantheon |
| Columbia University Press | Penguin |
| Cornell University Press | Pergamon |
| Crane Russak | Praeger |
| Crowell | Prentice-Hall |
| Dodd, Mead | Princeton University Press |
| Doubleday | Public Affairs |
| Dutton | Putnam |
| Farrar, Straus & Giroux | Rand |
| Follett | Random House |
| Foreign Policy Association | Regnery |
| Funk & Wagnalls | Rutgers University Press |
| George Washington University Press | Sage |
| Georgetown University. | St. Martin's |
|   Center for Strategic and | Scarecrow |
|   International Studies | Schocken |
| Harcourt Brace Jovanovich | Scribner |
| Harper & Row | Sijthoff & Noordhoff |
| Harvard University Press | Simon & Schuster |
| Heritage Foundation | Stackpole |
| Holt, Rinehart & Winston | Stanford University Press |
| Hoover Institution | Time-Life |
| Houghton Mifflin | U.S. Air University |
| International Institute for Strategic Studies | U.S. Govt. Print. Off. |
| International Publishers | University of California Press |
| Johns Hopkins University Press | University of Chicago Press |
| Knopf | University of Pennsylvania Press |
| Lippincott | Van Nostrand Reinhold |
| Little, Brown | Viking |
| Longman | Weidenfeld & Nicolson |
| McGraw-Hill | Westview |
| Macmillan | Wiley |
| MIT Press | Wilson |
| Monthly Review | World |
| Morrow | Yale University Press |

33

## Abbreviations

art., arts. ---------------------------------------------------- article, articles

cf. ante ------------------------------------------------------- compare above

cf. post ------------------------------------------------------- compare after

chap., chaps. ------------------------------------------------- chapter, chapters

comp., comps. ------------------------------------------------ compiler, compilers

dept. ---------------------------------------------------------- department

ed., eds. ------------------------------------------------------ editor, editors

ed. ------------------------------------------------------------ edition

ff. ------------------------------------------------------------- more than one page following

ibid. ----------------------------------------------------------- <u>ibidem</u> (in the same place)

n.d. ----------------------------------------------------------- no date

n.p. ----------------------------------------------------------- no place; no publisher

no., nos. ----------------------------------------------------- number, numbers

p., pp. -------------------------------------------------------- page, pages

par., pars. --------------------------------------------------- paragraph, paragraphs

pt., pts. ------------------------------------------------------- part, parts

ref. ----------------------------------------------------------- reference

rev. ed. ------------------------------------------------------- revised edition

sec., secs. ---------------------------------------------------- section, sections

trans. --------------------------------------------------------- translator

vol., vols. ---------------------------------------------------- volume, volumes

v.p. ----------------------------------------------------------- various paging

34

# CHAPTER IV

## SECURITY

Executive Order (E.O.) 12958, "Classified National Security Information" directs agencies to observe the democratic principles of openness and the free flow of information, as well as to enforce protective measures for safeguarding information critical to the national security.

The Department of the Navy Information Security Program Regulation (SECNAVINST 5510.36), which has provided the guidelines for marking classified material, has replaced OPNAVINST 5510.1H as the guide for information security. Sweeping changes instituted as a result of the new executive order have led to the development and implementation of the DOD Guide to Marking Classified Documents (DOD 5200.1-PH), effective in April 1997. All sources of information have been combined in this chapter in order to enable proper security classification of material as required today.

This chapter offers guidance to the proper security classification of written products if security classification is required. The body of the chapter contains pertinent excerpts from the Department of the Navy Information Security Program Regulation (DON ISPR)[4] (SECNAVINST 5510.36), the DOD Guide to Marking Classified Documents (DOD 5200.1-PH, April 1997), and Executive Order 12958, which are intended to give a basic picture of the classification process in effect today. All paragraph references and exhibits are to be found in the DON ISPR unless referenced to the DOD Guide or E.O. Pages 45-46 contain procedures that must be followed by authors in classification of their papers. Pages 47-48 provide a sample classification approval request form to be forwarded to the President/Security Manager recommending assignment of security classification to a paper. In the event there is a specific classification guide available for the topic undertaken (see page 49 for identification procedures), the reference given in the memorandum to support the classification may consist merely of the appropriate citation from that guide. All other procedures should be followed as described in this chapter. Appendix B offers a brief guide to the location of specific instructions and paragraphs in the DON ISPR that will further assist writers.

During the preliminary preparation of a classified written product, individuals must safeguard all output and working papers in accordance with security regulations at a level equivalent to that of the intended final classification. Because of the nature of working papers, markings on them need not be comprehensive. Specially marked folders or other appropriate containers should be utilized and properly secured to avoid security viola-tions. Remember, all classified material, including classified working papers must be stored in an authorized

---

[4] Hereafter referred to as the DON ISPR.

35

"classified security container" *only*, and destroyed according to procedures for disposing of classified information.

## CLASSIFICATION[5]

### 4-1 BASIC POLICY

1. EO 12958 is the only basis for classifying National Security Information, except as provided by reference Title 42, U.S. Code. It is DON policy to make available to the public as much information concerning its activities as possible, consistent with the need to protect national security. Therefore, information shall be classified only to protect national security.

2. Information classified by DON Original Classification Authorities (OCAS) shall be declassified as soon as it no longer meets the standards for classification in the interest of national security.

### 4-2 CLASSIFICATION LEVELS

1. Information that requires protection against unauthorized disclosure in the interest of national security shall be classified at the Top Secret, Secret, or Confidential levels. Except as otherwise provided by statute, no other terms shall be used to identify U.S. classified information. Terms such as 'For official Use Only" (FOUO) or "Secret Sensitive" (SS) shall not be used for the identification of U.S. classified information.

2. Top Secret is the classification level applied to information the unauthorized disclosure of which could reasonably be expected to cause exceptionally grave damage to national security. Examples include information, the unauthorized release of which could result in armed hostilities against the U.S. or its allies; a disruption of foreign relations vitally affecting the national security; the compromise of vital national defense plans; the disclosure of complex cryptographic and communication intelligence systems; the disclosure of sensitive intelligence operations; and the disclosure of significant scientific or technological developments vital to national security.

3. Secret is the classification level applied to information the unauthorized disclosure of which could reasonably be expected to cause serious damage to national security. Examples include information, the unauthorized release of which could result in the disruption of foreign relations significantly affecting the national security; the significant impairment of a program or policy directly related to the national security; the disclosure of significant military plans or intelligence operations; and the disclosure of scientific or technological developments relating to national security.

---

[5] All paragraph references are to the DON ISPR (SECNAVINST 5510.36) unless indicated from the DOD Guide to Marking (DOD 5200.1-PH).

36

4. _Confidential_ is the classification level applied to information the unauthorized disclosure of which could reasonably be expected to cause damage to national security. Examples include information, the unauthorized release of which could result in disclosure of ground, air, and naval forces (e.g., force levels and force dispositions); or disclosure of performance characteristics, such as design, test, and production data of U.S. munitions and weapon systems.

## 4-3 ORIGINAL CLASSIFICATION

Original classification is the initial decision that an item of information could be expected to cause damage to national security if subjected to unauthorized disclosure.

## 4-4 ORIGINAL CLASSIFICATION AUTHORITY (OCA)

The authority to originally classify information as Top Secret, Secret, or Confidential rests with the SECNAV and officials delegated such authority. The SECNAV personally designated certain officials to be Top Secret OCAS. The authority to originally classify information as Secret or Confidential is inherent in Top Secret original classification authority. OCAS are designated by virtue of their position. Original classification authority is not transferable and shall not be further delegated. Only the current incumbents of the positions listed in exhibit 4A of the DON ISPR have original classification authority. President, Naval War College is designated as a Top Secret OCA.

## 4-9 DERIVATIVE CLASSIFICATION

1. While original classification is the initial determination that information requires--in the interest of national security--protection against unauthorized disclosure, derivative classification is the incorporating, paraphrasing, restating, or generating in new form, information that is already classified. Derivative classification also includes the marking of newly developed information consistent with the classification markings that apply to the classified source. This encompasses the classification of information based on classification guidance or source documents, but not the mere duplication or reproduction of existing classified information. An estimated 99 percent of the classified information produced by DON commands is derivatively classified.

2. A derivative classifier shall:

a. Observe and respect the original classification determinations made by OCAS (and as codified in classified source documents and security classification guides);

b. Use caution when paraphrasing or restating information extracted from a classified source document to determine whether the classification may have been changed in the process;

37

c. Carry forward the pertinent classification markings to any newly created information.

6-2 DON COMMAND AND DATE OF ORIGIN

Every classified document shall indicate on the front cover, first page, or title page (hereafter referred to as the "face" of the document) the identity of the DON command that originated the document (a command's letterhead satisfies this requirement) and the date the document was originated.

6-3 OVERALL CLASSIFICATION LEVEL MARKING

Mark (stamp, print, or permanently affix with a sticker or tape) the face and back cover, top and bottom center, of all classified documents to show the highest overall classification level of the information they contain. These markings shall be conspicuous enough (i.e. larger than the text) to alert anyone handling the document that it is classified. Include an explanatory statement on the face of any classified document which cannot be marked in this manner.

6-4 INTERIOR PAGE MARKINGS

1. Mark each interior page of a document (except blank pages), top and bottom center, with the highest overall classification level of any information contained on the page (see paragraph 6-7, 6-11 and 6-12 (and exhibit 6A-1) for placement of certain warning notices and intelligence control markings on interior pages). If the page is printed front and back, mark both sides of the page. Mark pages containing only unclassified information "UNCLASSIFIED".

2. An alternative interior page marking method permits each page to be marked with the highest overall classification level of information contained in the document. Using this highest overall classification scheme for interior pages, however, does not eliminate the requirement to mark portions.

6-5 PORTION MARKINGS

1. Mark each portion (e.g., title, section, part, paragraph, or subparagraph) of a classified document to show its classification level. This requirement eliminates doubt as to which portions of a document are classified. Place the appropriate abbreviation ("TS" (Top Secret), "S" (Secret), "C" (Confidential) or "U" (Unclassified)) , immediately following the portion letter or number, or in the absence of letters or numbers, immediately before the beginning of the portion (see exhibit 6A-2). The abbreviation "FOUO may be used to designate unclassified portions containing information exempt from mandatory release to the public under SECNAVINST 5720.42E, DON Freedom of Information Act Program (see exhibit 6A-3 of the DON ISPR). Additionally, place the applicable abbreviated warning

38

notice(s) and intelligence control marking(s) directly after the abbreviated classification level of each portion.

2. If an exceptional situation makes individual portion markings clearly impracticable, place a statement on the face of the document describing which portions are classified, and at what classification level. This statement shall identify the classified information as specifically as would parenthetical portion markings.

3. Mark figures, tables, graphs, charts, and similar illustrations appearing within a document with their classification level, including the short form(s) of any applicable warning notice(s) and intelligence control marking(s). Place these markings within, or adjacent to, the figure, table, graph, or chart. Mark chart and graph captions or titles with the abbreviated classification level (including all applicable abbreviated warning notice(s) and intelligence control marking(s)) . When figure or table numbers are used to identify the captions or titles, place these abbreviated marking(s) after the number and before the text (see exhibit 6A-4 of the DON ISPR).

4. Portions of U.S. documents containing NATO or Foreign Government Iinformation shall be marked to reflect the country, international organization, and appropriate classification level (see exhibit 6A-5 of the DON ISPR). The letter "R" shall be used for the identification of NATO RESTRICTED or Foreign Government RESTRICTED information.

6-6 SUBJECTS AND TITLES

1. Mark subjects or titles with the appropriate abbreviated classification level, after the subject or title (see exhibits 6A-2, 6A-3 and 6A-5 of the DON ISPR). When subjects or titles of classified documents are included in the reference line, enclosure line, or the body of information, the classification of the subject or title shall follow.

2. Whenever possible, subjects or titles shall be unclassified for identification and reference purposes. If a classified subject or title is unavoidable, an unclassified short title shall be added for reference purposes, for example:

e.g. Subj : ASW OPERATIONS IN THE BATAVIAN LITTORAL ON 2 JUNE 99 (C) (SHORT TITLE: 'ASWOPS 3-99 (U))

6-7 PLACEMENT OF ASSOCIATED MARKINGS

1. Associated markings are spelled out in their entirety on the face of a document. Certain associated markings, (e.g., the "Classified by," "Reason," "Derived from," "Downgrade to," and "Declassify on," lines) , and certain warning notices (e.g., RD, CNWDI and PRO) are placed on the face of the document in the lower left hand corner (see exhibit 6A-l of the DON ISPR). Other warning notices (e.g., dissemination and reproduction notices, SIOP-ESI and CRYPTO) and all intelligence control markings, are spelled out in their entirety on the face of the document, at the bottom center of the page, above the classification level

39

marking. See paragraph 6-23 of the <u>DON ISPR</u> for the proper placement of markings on correspondence and letters of transmittal.

2. Associated markings are not spelled out on interior pages. However, the short forms of Certain Warning notice(s), (e.g., "RESTRICTED DATA," "FORMERLY RESTRICTED DATA," "NNPI," and "CRYPTO"), and the short form of <u>all</u> intelligence control marking(s), applicable to each page, shall be marked after the classification level at the bottom center of each page. Associated markings shall not be placed on the back cover of any classified document (see exhibit 6A-1of the <u>DON ISPR</u>) .

<u>DOD GUIDE: ORIGINAL CLASSIFICATION/DECLASSIFICATION MARKINGS</u>

1. All classified material will be marked with the following standard markings:

Classified by: _____ (See Note 1)

Reason: _____ (See Note 2)

Declassify on: _____ (See Note 3)

2. U.S. documents containing foreign government information will be marked as follows:

Derived from: _____ (See Note 4)

Declassify on: _____ (See Note 4)

NOTE 1. If the document is original classification, the identification of the original classification authority will be inserted. If the document is derivative classification, the identity of the security classification guide, source document, or other authority for classification will be inserted following "Derived from:" vice "Classified by:". If more than one source is applicable, the words <u>Multiple Sources</u> will be inserted.

NOTE 2. The original classifier shall identify a concise reason for classification that, at a minimum, cites the applicable classification categories in section 1.5 of E.O. 12958 as a basis for classification. Information may not be considered for classification unless it concerns the following categories:

     a. Military plans, weapons systems, or operations.

     b. Foreign government information.

     c. Intelligence activities (including special activities), intelligence sources or methods, or cryptology.

d. Foreign relations or foreign activities of the United States, including confidential sources.

e. Scientific, technological, or economic matters relating to the national security.

f. U.S. Government programs for safeguarding nuclear materials or facilities.

g. Vulnerabilities or capabilities of systems, installations, projects or plans relating to the national security.

NOTE 3. See pages 43-44 of this chapter, "Declassify on Line" and "Exemption Categories."

NOTE 4. The U.S. Government affords protection to information provided by foreign governments. Care must be taken to identify the source of the information. The "Derived From" line should cite the title of the document. The declassification date, event, or exemption category is carried forward to the "Declassify on" line, if known.

e.g., Derived from: FGI Source Document or Identify Foreign Government Source
    Document dated _____

Declassify on: X5, FGI

When the identity of the country must be concealed, substitute "Foreign Government Information (FGI)" for the name of the country and note the country in the record copy of the document.

Mark the portions that contain the foreign government information to indicate the country of origin and the classification level, e.g., (FGI-C), (UK-S).

Include the following statement at the bottom of documents containing classified FGI: "This document contains (country of origin) Information."

## DOD GUIDE: DERIVATIVE CLASSIFICATION--CONVERTING OLD DOWNGRAD-ING/DECLASSIFICATION MARKINGS TO NEWLY CREATED DOCUMENTS

Newly created material that derives its classification from a source document classified, or a security classification guide promulgated prior to 1 August 1982, will be treated as follows:

1. Identify the source used as the basis for classification on the "Derived from" line of the derivative document.

41

2. If the source document bears, or the security classification guide specifies a declassification date or event, the date or event will be carried forward to the newly created material, to the "Declassify on" line of the derivative document.

3. When the "Declassify on" line of the source document is marked "Originating Agency's Determination Required" or "OADR", mark the "Declassify on" line of the derivative document to indicate:

        a. The fact that the source document is marked "OADR"

        b. The date of origin of the source document.

This marking will permit future determination when classified information becomes 25 years old. If the information is determined to be of permanent historic value, provisions of the automatic declassification program (section 3.4 of E.O. 12958) apply: e.g., Derived from: ASD(C3I) Memorandum. Subj: Classification Markings (U)

        Declassify on: Source document marked "OADR"
                    Date of source 6/25/94

## DOD GUIDE: DERIVATIVE CLASSIFICATION-CONVERTING FROM MULTIPLE SOURCES

When using more than one classified source document in creating a derivative document portion or paragraph, mark the classified information incorporated in the derivative document with the classification level indicated on the source documents. Enter "Multiple Sources" on the "Derived from" line of the derived document to indicate that more than one classified source was used.

NOTE: For a source document marked "Multiple Sources", the "Multiple Sources" notation will not be carried forward to the new document since the actual sources of classification could not be traced. Instead, identify the source document by the originator, date, and subject on the "Derived from" line of the derivative (your) document.

| |
|---|
| Classified by:Multiple Sources<br>Declassify on:OADR<br><br>**SECRET** |

**Derivative Document used as a Source Document**

| |
|---|
| Derived from: ASD(C3I) Memo; Subject:<br>Security Awareness of Classified Markings (U)<br>Declassify on: Source marked OADR<br>dated July 25, 1995<br><br>**SECRET** |

**Derivative Document**

Maintain the identification of all classified sources with the file or record copy of the derivative document.  If practicable, include the list with all copies of the derivative document (to be listed on NAVWARCOL FORM 5510.2 REV 7/97).

**Official File Copy**

Derived from: Multiple Sources

|       | **Source** | **ASD(C3I) Memo dtd** |
|-------|-----------|------------------------|
| **1:** |           | **Oct 15, 95; Subj: _____** |
|       |           | **Declassify on: X-6** |
|       | **Source 2:** | **SECDEF Memo dtd** |
|       |           | **July 1, 94; Subj: _____** |
|       |           | **Declassify on: OADR** |

## DOD GUIDE:  "DECLASSIFY ON LINE" AND "EXEMPTION CATEGORIES"

When determining the duration of classification, choose one of the following three declassification instructions:  (Whenever possible, select the declassification instruction that will result in the shortest duration of classification.)

### 1.  Date or Event

When possible, identify the date or event for declassification that corresponds to the lapse of the information's national security sensitivity.  The date or event shall not exceed 10 years from the date of the original classification e.g.

Classified by:Emmet Paige
ASD (C3I)
Reason: 1.5(a) and (d)
Declassify on: December 31, 2002
or
Declassify on: Completion of Operation

**OR**

### 2.  Ten Year Duration

When a specific date or event cannot be determined, identify the date that is 10 years from the date of the original classification

**OR**

### 3.  Exemptions from the Ten Year Rule

43

If the information has been determined exempt from declassification at 10 years by the original classifier, place the letter "X" plus a brief recitation of the exemption category(ies) OR the letter "X" plus the corresponding number to that exemption category(ies) in section 1.6(d) of Executive Order 12958.

## E.O. 12958

## Section 1.6(d) "Exemption Categories"

## Exemption from 10-year Declassification

| Marking | |
| --- | --- |
| X1. | Reveal an intelligence source, method, or activity, or a cryptologic system or activity. |
| X2. | Reveal information that would assist in the development or use of weapons of mass destruction. |
| X3. | Reveal information that would impair the development or use of technology within a United States weapons system. |
| X4. | Reveal United States military plans or national security emergency preparedness plans. |
| X5. | Reveal foreign government information. |
| X6. | Damage relations between the United States and a foreign government, reveal a confidential source, or seriously undermine diplomatic activities that are reasonably expected to be ongoing for a period greater than 10 years. |
| X7. | Impair the ability of responsible United States Government officials to protect the President, the Vice President, and other individuals for whom protection services, in the interest of national security, are authorized. |
| X8. | Violate a statute, treaty or international agreement. |

44

6-11 <u>WARNING NOTICES</u>

1. Warning notices advise the holders of a document of additional protective measures such as restrictions on reproduction, dissemination or extraction. Placement of warning notices is shown in page 6A-9 of the <u>DON ISPR</u>.

8-8 <u>DISSEMINATION OF TECHNICAL DOCUMENTS</u>

1. Originators within a command who are responsible for technical documents must determine the extent to which the documents are available for distribution, release, and dissemination without additional approvals or authorizations, and mark them accordingly.

2. All newly generated unclassified technical documents must bear one of the distribution statements described in Exhibit 8A of the <u>DON ISPR</u>. Existing unclassified technical documents, including informal documents such as working papers, memoranda, and preliminary reports will be assigned a distribution statement from Exhibit 8A if they are not already in the public domain and if they are likely to be disseminated outside the Department of Defense. Existing technical documents do not have to be reviewed for the sole purpose of assigning distribution statements; but when they are withdrawn from files for use, it must be determined whether distribution limitations are necessary and, if so, they must be marked accordingly.

3. Classified technical documents shall be assigned distribution statement B, C, D, E, or F from Exhibit 8B of the <u>DON ISPR</u>. The distribution statement assigned to a classified document shall be retained on the document after its declassification or until specifically changed or removed by the originating command. Technical documents that are declassified and have no distribution statement assigned shall be handled as distribution statement F documents until changed by the originating command.

<u>Procedures for Obtaining Approval of Security Classification of Research Papers</u>

1. Papers and reports in draft form will be treated as Working Papers, and marked with the highest classification of any information contained in the document. When using a classified document, record the classifier and declassification data on initial use to avoid having to re-check sources. The center or academic department of origin will determine which documents will be selected for retention in Naval War College files or sent to commands or activities outside the Naval War College as formal documents.

2. The classification and downgrading/declassification of a formal document must be approved. Original classification of SECRET, CONFIDENTIAL, and TOP SECRET must be approved by the President, Naval War College. Derivative classification of SECRET and CONFIDENTIAL must be approved by the Security Manager.

45

3.  The writer will forward the original copy of the formal document, with all proper security markings, to the President/Security Manager.  Submission will be by request form to the President or Security Manager, as appropriate.  (See pages 47-48 for a sample form.)

4.  After classification is approved, the endorsed memorandum will be retained by the Security Manager.  The original document will be transferred to library custody by the chairmen of the academic departments via Head, Mail and File Branch, in accordance with the provisions of Naval War College Standard Organization and Regulations Manual.  Sufficient copies to provide for distribution and deposit in the Defense Technical Information Center will also be transferred to library custody.  (See Chapter V.)

DATE:

# REQUEST FOR APPROVAL OF SECURITY CLASSIFICATION

1. NAME:          RANK          FIRST          MI          LAST          SERVICE

2. DEPARTMENT/ORGANIZATION (CHECK ONE)

   ☐ FACULTY          ☐ CNWS          ☐ CNC&S          ☐ OTHER _____
                                                                    (SPECIFY)

3. DOCUMENT TITLE:

4. REQUIREMENT OF: (SPECIFIC ACADEMIC DEPARTMENT, CENTER FOR ADVANCED RESEARCH, ETC.)

5. CLASSIFICATION REQUESTED FOR THIS DOCUMENT:

   ☐ TOP SECRET              ☐ SECRET          ☐ CONFIDENTIAL
   ☐ RESTRICTED DATA         ☐ NOFORN          ☐ OTHER _____
                                                           (SPECIFY)

6. CLASSIFICATION OF THIS DOCUMENT IS:

   ☐ DERIVATIVE              ☐ ORIGINAL

   NOTE: DOCUMENTS DRAWING ON CLASSIFIED SOURCES FOR THEIR CLASSIFICATION LEVEL ARE CONSIDERED
         "DERIVATIVE" AS ARE DOCUMENTS WHICH ARE CLASSIFIED BASED ON PUBLISHED CLASSIFICATION GUIDES.

7. SOURCES:

   ATTACH COPIES OF THE TITLE PAGES OF ALL SOURCES WITH DOWNGRADING INDICATED, OR FILL OUT SECTION 7
   ON REVERSE SIDE.

8. DOWNGRADING INSTRUCTIONS FOR THIS DOCUMENT

   CLASSIFIED BY/OR DERIVED FROM: _____
   REASON: _____
   DECLASSIFY ON: _____

9. SIGNATURE OF REQUESTOR:

10. APPROVAL BY SECURITY MANAGER: (DERIVATIVE CLASSIFICATION)/PRESIDENT, NAVAL WAR COLLEGE
    (ORIGINAL CLASSIFICATION):

    ☐ APPROVED:               ☐ DISAPPROVED FOR THE CLASSIFICATION OF:

    _____

    THE DOWNGRADING AND DECLASSIFICATION INSTRUCTIONS RECOMMENDED IN BLOCK 8 SHALL BE USED.

    _____
    (SIGNATURE)

    POC 29

47

7.  SOURCES (CONTINUED)

ALL INFORMATION BELOW SHOULD BE FOUND ON THE TITLE PAGE OF SOURCE DOCUMENTS.

A.  TITLE _____

OVERALL CLASSIFICATION _____

ORIGINATOR _____

SOURCE CLASSIFIED BY _____

DECLASSIFY ON (OADR, DATE OR EXEMPTION) _____

DATE OF PUBLICATION (IF AVAILABLE) _____

- - - - - - - - - - - - - - - - - - - - - - - - - - - - - - - - - - - - - - - - - - - - - - - - - - - - -

B.  TITLE _____

OVERALL CLASSIFICATION _____

ORIGINATOR _____

SOURCE CLASSIFIED BY _____

DECLASSIFY ON (OADR, DATE OR EXEMPTION) _____

DATE OF PUBLICATION (IF AVAILABLE) _____

- - - - - - - - - - - - - - - - - - - - - - - - - - - - - - - - - - - - - - - - - - - - - - - - - - - - -

C.  TITLE _____

OVERALL CLASSIFICATION _____

ORIGINATOR _____

SOURCE CLASSIFIED BY _____

DECLASSIFY ON (OADR, DATE OR EXEMPTION) _____

DATE OF PUBLICATION (IF AVAILABLE) _____

- - - - - - - - - - - - - - - - - - - - - - - - - - - - - - - - - - - - - - - - - - - - - - - - - - - - -

D.  TITLE _____

OVERALL CLASSIFICATION _____

ORIGINATOR _____

SOURCE CLASSIFIED BY _____

DECLASSIFY ON (OADR, DATE OR EXEMPTION) _____

DATE OF PUBLICATION (IF AVAILABLE) _____

48

Additional Information

        Classification Guide          Consult OPNAVINST 5513.1 series

        Joint Chiefs of Staff Papers   Consult JCS Memorandum of policy 39, <u>Release Procedures for JCS Papers</u>.

*NOTE: All personnel are reminded that <u>all</u> classified information is regarded as not releasable to any foreign nation or person until an authorized foreign disclosure official makes a positive determination that a foreign release is warranted.

49

# CHAPTER V

## DISTRIBUTION, PUBLICATION, AND DEPOSIT OF STUDENT AND ADVANCED RESEARCH PAPERS AND PRIZE ESSAYS

Papers prepared for the Naval War College are considered to belong to the College. Policies for distribution and for commercial publication of student academic and research papers are outlined in the NWC Standard Organization and Regulations Manual and in the references therein. This chapter outlines procedures for forwarding student papers, research reports, and prize essays selected by the academic departments, the Center for Naval Warfare Studies, and the Office of the Dean of Academics for deposit in the Library and in the Defense Technical Information Center or the Fleet Tactical Library.

In accordance with the provisions of the NWC Standard Organization and Regulations Manual governing awards and prizes; the academic departments, the Center for Naval Warfare Studies, and the Office of the Dean of Academics forward the original copies of selected research papers and prize essays to the Library for archival purposes. Additional copies are forwarded for distribution to Department of Defense activities named by the dean or chairman of the respective center or department and for deposit in the Defense Technical Information Center.

Library and Defense Technical Information Center requirements for papers are outlined below:

1. Copies

    Library--the original copy of an unpublished work.

    Distribution by the Library--sufficient copies to forward to the list of addressees.

    Defense Technical Information Center deposit--both classified and unclassified papers, two copies with completed DD Form 1473 including an unclassified abstract (not exceeding 200 words).

2. Title page--complete information as shown in the samples in Appendix A.

3. Incomplete papers, reproduced (not original) copies of papers, proof copies of books, papers which do not comply with provisions of the Security Manual, etc., will not be accepted for NWC Library or Defense Technical Information Center deposit or for distribution to Department of Defense activities. Such papers will be either returned to the center/department or forwarded to the Naval War College Archives.

Distribution of research papers and prize essays will be accomplished by the Library Director at the time of deposit. Copies will be deposited in the Defense Technical Information Center so that future requests for them can be forwarded to the center for

50

action. The cover and title page of research papers and essays must show any distribution statement controlling the availability of the paper in accordance with Exhibit 12B in the Security Manual.

Specific instances of distribution limitations are: (a) unclassified papers and essays that contain references to classified sources may carry a distribution statement <u>other</u> than "A," in order to prevent release to the public; the student and his/her faculty supervisor shall determine whether the paper should have Distribution Statement A or B. (b) classified papers containing classified intelligence information including NOFORN must carry Distribution Statement E (distribution authorized to DOD components only (DOD Instruction 5230.22 series) or F including NOFORN/WNINTEL (further dissemination only as directed by originating Naval War College Department or higher DOD authority).

Sample memos for forwarding classified and unclassified research papers and essays to the Library and a copy of the Report Documentation Page appear on pages 54-56.

51

<u>S A M P L E</u>

<u>UNCLASSIFIED TRANSMITTAL FORM</u>

<u>DATE</u>:

<u>MEMORANDUM</u>

From: Chairman/Dean _____
To:     Library Director (Code E-a)

Subj:  Unclassified Research Papers/Essay; Transmittal of

Ref:    (a) NWC SORM


1. The research paper/essay _____[Title and Author]_____

_____

_____

is hereby forwarded with sufficient copies for:

    (1) Library deposit--(original copy).

    (2) Distribution to the attached addressee list.

    (3)Deposit in DTIC--(2 copies and DD Form 1473 with  distribution statement, key words, and abstract provided in blocks 3, 18, and 19).


                                        _____
                                             Signature

52

SAMPLE

CLASSIFIED TRANSMITTAL FORM

DATE

MEMORANDUM

From: Chairman/Dean _____
To:    Library Director (Code E-111)

Subj: Classified Research Papers/Essay; Transmittal of

Ref:   (a) NWC SORM

1. The research paper/essay _____[Title, Author, and Classification]]___

_____

_____

is hereby forwarded with sufficient copies for:

    (1) Library deposit--(original copy).

    (2) Distribution to the attached addressee list.

    (3)Deposit in DTIC--(2 copies and DD Form 1473 with distribution statement, key words, and abstract provided in blocks 3, 18, and 19).

_____
Signature

53

## REPORT DOCUMENTATION PAGE

| | |
|---|---|
| **1. Report Security Classification**: UNCLASSIFIED | |
| **2. Security Classification Authority:** | |
| **3. Declassification/Downgrading Schedule:** | |
| **4. Distribution/Availability of Report:  DISTRIBUTION STATEMENT A:  APPROVED FOR PUBLIC RELEASE; DISTRIBUTION IS UNLIMITED.** | |
| **5. Name of Performing Organization:** **JOINT MILITARY OPERATIONS DEPARTMENT** | |

| **6. Office Symbol:** C | **7. Address:** **NAVAL WAR COLLEGE** **686 CUSHING ROAD** **NEWPORT, RI  02841-1207** |
|---|---|

| | |
|---|---|
| **8. Title** (Include Security Classification): | |
| **9. Personal Authors**: | |

| **10. Type of Report**:  FINAL | **11. Date of Report**: |
|---|---|

| | |
|---|---|
| **12. Page Count**: | |
| **13. Supplementary Notation:**   A paper submitted to the Faculty of the NWC in partial satisfaction of the requirements of the JMO Department.  The contents of this paper reflect my own personal views and are not necessarily endorsed by the NWC or the Department of the Navy. | |
| **14. Ten key words that relate to your paper:** | |
| **15. Abstract:** | |

| **16. Distribution / Availability of Abstract:** | Unclassified X | Same As Rpt | DTIC Users |
|---|---|---|---|

| | |
|---|---|
| **17. Abstract Security Classification:**  UNCLASSIFIED | |
| **18. Name of Responsible Individual:**  CHAIRMAN, JOINT MILITARY OPERATIONS DEPARTMENT | |

| **19. Telephone:**  841-XXXX | **20. Office Symbol:**       1C |
|---|---|

Security Classification of This Page Unclassified

54

## Instructions for Preparation of Report Documentation Page

1. All information should be typed.

2. Security Classification of the Form:

    a. This form should be unclassified if possible.

    b. In accordance with security program regulations, classification markings are to be stamped, printed, or written at the top and bottom of the form in capital letters that are larger than those used in the text of the document.

    c. Unclassified abstracts and titles describing classified documents may appear separately from the documents in an unclassified context; e.g., in Defense Technical Information Center (DTIC) announcement bulletins and bibliographies. this must be considered in the preparation and marking of unclassified abstracts and titles.

3. Specific Blocks:

    Block 1: Report Security Classification: The highest security classification contained in the report.

    Block 2: Security Classification Authority: Leave blank.

    Block 3: Declassification/Downgrading Schedule: Leave blank.

    Block 4: Distribution/Availability of Report: For classified report, leave blank. For unclassified report fill in: DISTRIBUTION STATEMENT A: APPROVED FOR PUBLIC RELEASE; DISTRIBUTION IS UNLIMITED.

    Block 5: Name of Performing Organization: Either: Joint Military Operations Department, National Security Decision Making Department, Strategy and Policy Department, Electives Program, College of Continuing Education, Naval Command College, Naval Staff College, or Center for Naval Warfare Studies.

    Block 6: Office Symbol: Either "NWC Code 1A" for Strategy and Policy Department, "NWC Code 1B" for National Security Decision Making Department, "NWC Code 1C" for Joint Military Operations Department, "NWC Code 1D" for the Electives Program, "NWC Code 1G" for the College of Continuing Education, "NWC 1H" for the Naval Command College, "NWC 1J" for the Naval Staff College, or NWC Code 3" for the Center for Naval Warfare Studies.

    Block 7: Address: Insert:  Naval War College
                        686 Cushing Road
                        Newport, R.I. 02841-1207

    Block 8: Title: Insert full title of paper or report, including classification of the title as appropriate.

    Block 9: Personal Author(s): Full name and rank or title of author(s).

    Block 10: Type of Report: Insert "FINAL"

    Block 11: Date of Report: Insert date on cover.

    Block 12: Page count:

55

Block 13: Supplementary Notation: Insert: A paper submitted to _____ [the faculty of the Naval War College, or to the Director of the Advanced Research Department in the Center for Naval Warfare Studies] in partial satisfaction of the departmental requirements [or of the requirements for the Masters of Arts Degree in National Security and Strategic Studies].
The contents of this paper reflect my own personal views and are not necessarily endorsed by the Naval War College or the Department of the Navy.

Block 14: Ten key words that relate to your paper: Self-explanatory.

Block 15: Abstract: Abbreviate the abstract as necessary to fit in block 15.

Block 16: Distribution / Availability of Abstract: Mark appropriate boxes.

Block 17: Abstract Security Classification: As appropriate.

Block 18: Name of Responsible Individual: Title of the chairman or director of the organization shown in Block 5; e.g., Chairman, National Decision Making Department

Block 19: Telephone: Telephone number of responsible individual of Block 18.

Block 20: Office Symbol: Office symbol of responsible individual of Block 18.

56

# APPENDIX A

# EXAMPLES

NAVAL WAR COLLEGE
Newport, R.I.

TITLE OF PAPER

by

Name
Rank and Service

A paper submitted to the Faculty of the Naval War College in partial satisfaction of the requirements of the Department of [National Security Decision Making].

The contents of this paper reflect my own personal views and are not necessarily endorsed by the Naval War College or the Department of the Navy.

Signature: _____

16 May 2000
[Date of submission of paper.]

_____

[Typed name of Faculty Advisor and Academic Title]

*If distribution of paper is limited in accordance with the DON ISPR, show Distribution Statement here.

A-2

CLASSIFICATION

NAVAL WAR COLLEGE
Newport, R.I.

<u>TITLE OF PAPER</u>

by

Name
Rank and Service

A paper submitted to the Faculty of the Naval War College in partial satisfaction of the requirements of the Department of [Joint Military Operations].

The contents of this paper reflect my own personal views and are not necessarily endorsed by the Naval War College or the Department of the Navy.

Signature: _____

16 May 2000
[Date of submission of paper.]

_____
Faculty Advisor
[Typed name of Faculty Advisor and Academic Title]

[Warnings or notices as applicable.]
Classified by Multiple Sources
Declassify on 31 December 19XX (or OADR, as applicable)
Approved by Security Manager, Naval War College.

*If distribution of paper is limited in accordance with the DON <u>ISPR</u>, show Distribution Statement here.

A-3

NAVAL WAR COLLEGE
Newport, R.I.

TITLE OF PAPER

by

Name

Rank and Service

As an Advanced Research Project

A paper submitted to the Director of the Advanced Research Department in the Center for Naval Warfare Studies in partial satisfaction of the requirements for the Master of Arts Degree in National Security and Strategic Studies.

The contents of this paper reflect my own personal views and are not necessarily endorsed by the Naval War College or the Department of the Navy.

Signature: _____

16 May 2000
[Date of submission of paper.]

_____
Faculty Advisor
[Typed name of Faculty Advisor and Academic Title]

*If distribution of paper is limited in accordance with the DON ISPR, show Distribution Statement here.

A-4

Abstract

FACING A NUCLEAR-ARMED ADVERSARY IN A REGIONAL CONTINGENCY:

IMPLICATIONS FOR THE JOINT COMMANDER

Among the challenges facing the United States military in the post-Cold War world, none would be more difficult or complex than facing a nuclear-armed adversary in a regional contingency. One needs only to read today's headlines to acknowledge the validity of this threat and to contemplate the responsibilities and risks that would be borne by a joint commander required to engage such an adversary.

The possibility of nuclear use will complicate campaign planning, affect the course of action development and selection, and alter conventional warfighting doctrine and operations. The impact will be felt, at a minimum, in civil-military relations, coalition and alliance formation and maintenance, public opinion, media relations, associations with other states with weapons of mass destruction capability, intelligence assessment, rules of engagement, post-war considerations, force deployment and logistics, dispersal and posturing of forces, and active and passive defense. In brief, the sweep of potential consequences is very broad.

The time is now for joint commanders seriously to consider and prepare for the nasty business of engaging a nuclear-armed regional adversary. Presidential tasking and deterrence credibility demand it. Ignoring it will not make it disappear.

# APPENDIX B

# CHECKLIST FOR PREPARING CLASSIFIED DOCUMENTS

B-1

# CHECKLIST FOR PREPARING CLASSIFIED DOCUMENTS

Reference:   (a) SECNAVINST 5510.36 (DON Information and Personnel Security Program Regulation)

          (b) DOD 5200.1-PH (DOD Guide to Marking Classified Documents, April 1997)

          (c) Executive Order 12958 ("Classified National Security Information" 1995)

1. References (a), (b) and (c) provide guidance on preparing and marking unclassified and classified documents. Use the following checklist to ensure requirements have been met. Numbers in parentheses refer to paragraphs in reference (a) unless otherwise indicated.

## A. COVER OF DOCUMENT

1. --- Overall classification (including short form of Intelligence Control Markings) must appear in bold stamp (larger type than rest of print on cover page) centered at the top and bottom of the cover. The classification of the document must be as high as the highest classification of any information used in the paper. (para 6-3, Exhibit 6A-1)

2. --- Title must be marked; i.e., (U), (C), (S), (TS), (S-NF), etc. at end of title. (para 6-4)

3. --- Date of Preparation. (Exhibit 6A-1)

4. --- Name and Address of Preparing Activity (i.e., Naval War College, Newport, RI 02841) (para 6-2, Exhibit 6A-1)

5. --- Classified By: (For derivative classification, the identity of the security classification guide, source document or other authority for classification will be inserted following "Derived from:" vice "Classified by:". If more than one source used, the words Multiple Sources will be inserted). Placed at the bottom left corner of cover. Listing of Source/Multiple Sources (including agency and office of origin, overall classification and declassification date or event, any downgrading action required for each source document) will be provided to the Security Manager. (DOD Guide pp. 4 and 15; pp. 44-45 of this guide)

6. --- Reason: Original classification decisions shall state reason(s) for classifying as described in the categories specified in Section 1.5 of E.O. 12958. (Refer to pp. 44-45 of this guide)

7. --- Declassify On: (i.e., declassification date or event which shall not exceed 10 years from the date of the original classification; or, if no specified date or event identify the date that is 10 years from the date of the original classification; or, indicate exemption(s) from the 10 year rule (Exemptions as listed in Section 1.6(d) of E.O.

B-2

12958). (Refer to p. 49 of this guide) When the "Declassify on" line of the source document is marked "Originating Agency's Determination Required" or "OADR", mark the "Declassify on" line of the derivative document to indicate the fact the source document is marked "OADR" followed by the date of origin of the source document; e.g.,

> Declassify on: Source document marked "OADR"
> Date of source 6/25/94

> Note: "OADR" is not an approved marking for documents originally classified under E.O. 12958 (after 14 October 1995).

8. --- Warning Notices (e.g., RESTRICTED DATA; FORMERLY RESTRICTED DATA) at lower left. Refer to reference (a). Full notice required, no abbreviated or short form. (para 6-11, Exhibit 6A-9)

9. --- Intelligence Control Markings (e.g., CAUTION--PROPRIETARY INFORMATION INVOLVED; NOT RELEASABLE TO FOREIGN NATIONALS, etc.) at bottom center above classification marking. Refer to reference (a) for complete listing of Intelligence Control Markings. Full marking required, no abbreviated or short form. (para 6-12) Note: "WINTEL" AND "NO CONTRACT" are no longer in use, however, those documents created prior to 12 April 1995 having these markings continue to be not releasable to contractors until requirements of paragraph 6.1 of DCID 1/7 of 16 Apr 96 (NOTAL) are met.

10. --- Distribution Statement for newly generated unclassified or classified technical documents is placed at bottom left corner. Refer to reference (a) for criteria and complete listing of distribution statements. (Exhibit 8A)

B. TITLE PAGE (IF ANY)

1. --- Overall classification (including short form of Intelligence Control Markings) must appear in bold stamp (larger type than rest of print on title page) centered at the top and bottom of the title page. (para 6-6, Exhibit 6A-1)

2. --- Title must be marked; i.e., (U), (C), (S), (TS), (S-NF), etc. at end of title. (para 6-6)

3. --- Intelligence Control Markings (e.g., CAUTION--PROPRIETARY INFORMATION INVOLVED; NOT RELEASABLE TO FOREIGN NATIONALS, etc.) at bottom center above classification marking. Refer to reference (a) for complete listing of Intelligence Control Markings. Full marking required, no abbreviated or short form. (para 6-12; Exhibit 6A9-6A10-6A11)

B-3

4. --- Distribution Statement for newly generated <u>unclassified or classified technical documents</u> is placed at bottom left corner. Refer to reference (a) for criteria and complete listing of distribution statements. (Exhibit 8A)

## C. INTERIOR PAGES (PRINTING ON 1 SIDE OF PAGE ONLY)

1. --- The classification of each interior page (except blank pages) of a publication will be marked at the top and bottom center of the page and is based on the highest classification level of information contained on the page. *The overall classification of the publication is no longer used when marking internal pages of a document.*

   NOTE: If printing on FRONT AND BACK of each page, mark both sides of page with the highest classification of either side. The side with the lower classification should be indicated at the bottom with the statement "This page is Unclassified" or other classification as appropriate. The short form of any intelligence control marking that applies to information on a page is placed after the classification at the top and bottom. (Exhibit 9H)

2. --- Intelligence Control Markings (e.g., CAUTION--PROPRIETARY INFORMATION INVOLVED; NOT RELEASABLE TO FOREIGN NATIONALS, etc.) at bottom center above classification marking on the first page only. Refer to reference (a) for complete listing of Intelligence Control Markings. Full marking is required; no abbreviated or short forms are permitted. (para 6-12)

3. --- Mark each portion (e.g., paragraph, subparagraph, bullets if they express complete thoughts), titles, headings, captions, etc. with (U), (C), (S), (TS) and applicable abbreviated Warning Notices and Intelligence Control Markings (e.g., S-RD; S-NF). (para 6-5)

4. --- Mark any blank, unnumbered interior pages with the statement "This page is intentionally left blank."

5. --- Mark at the top and bottom of the page the overall classification of the page if all portions on that page are the same classification (i.e., "This page is Confidential" or "This page is Unclassified"). (para 6-3)

6. --- Subject headings and titles will be marked with the appropriate abbreviated symbol (i.e., (TS), (S), (C), (U), (S-NF), etc.). (para 6-6)

7. --- Figures, tables, graphs, charts, photographs, reduced computer printouts, and similar illustrations will be marked. The classification marking (including short form of intelligence control markings and warning notices) will be centered just below, above or within the illustration. Captions for illustrations will be marked separately with the abbreviated classification marking (including intelligence control markings

B-4

or other warning notices in their abbreviated form) preceding the text of the caption. (para 6-5; exhibit 6A4).

8. --- Mark classified major components (e.g., annexes, appendices) as individual documents. If an entire major component is unclassified, the first page of component may be marked at the top and bottom with the designation UNCLASSIFIED and a statement included such as "All portions of this (annex, appendix) are UNCLASSIFIED." When this method is used no further markings are required on the remaining pages of an unclassified major component. (para 6-21)

D. BACK COVER

1. --- Not required.

2. --- If not used, classified text may not appear on the reverse side of last page.

3. --- If not used, overall classification is placed at the top and bottom center of the reverse side of last page.

2. EXAMPLES OF MARKINGS:

| Full Marking | Short Form | Abbreviated Form |
|---|---|---|
| Top Secret/Secret | | (TS)/(S) |
| Confidential | | (C) |
| Unclassified | | (U) |
| Caution - Proprietary Information Involved | PROPIN | (PR) |
| Not Releasable to Foreign Nationals | NOFORN | (NF) |
| This Information Has Been Releasable to _____(Insert country (ies) | REL TO _____ | (REL _____) |
| Dissemination and Extraction of Information Controlled by Originator | ORCON | (OC) |
| Restricted Data This material contains Restricted Data as defined in the Atomic Energy Act of 1954. Unauthorized disclosure subject to administrative and criminal sanctions. | RESTRICTED DATA | (RD) |

B-5

Formerly Restricted Data
Unauthorized disclosure subject to
administrative and criminal sanctions. Handle
as Restricted Data in foreign dissemination.
Section 144.p, Atomic Energy Act of 1954

FORMERLY
RESTRICTED DATA

(FRD)

3. <u>Sources</u>. For approval of paper classifications, enclosure (1) must be completed and submitted to the Security Manager, along with a copy of the paper. Since a listing of sources with their downgrading instructions is required, it is best either to reproduce the title pages of all classified documents cited, or to fill out the form as research is being performed. Much time can be saved by completing these steps as research is accomplished.

4. The requirement for proper marking of classified documents, and for a listing of all sources, is not only a NAVWARCOL requirement; the information herein is taken from SECNAV and DOD sources. So long as classified documents can be compromised, the above is essential in order to properly safeguard information of limited distribution.

B-6

# THE RESEARCH PAPER: AN ANNOTATED BIBLIOGRAPHY

<u>Research Process</u>

Adler, Mortimer J. and Charles Van Doren.  <u>How to Read a Book</u>.  rev. ed.  New York:
    Simon and Schuster, 1972.
    Both a how-to book and a literary experience at the same time.

Allen, George R.  <u>The Graduate Students' Guide to Theses and Dissertations; A Practical
    Manual for Writing and Research</u>.  San Francisco:  Jossey-Bass, 1974.

Barzun, Jacques and Henry F. Graff.  <u>The Modern Researcher</u>.  4th ed.  San Diego:  Harcourt
    Brace Jovanovich, 1985.
    Discusses research technique, writing style and format of research paper.

Berkman, Robert I.  <u>Find It Fast:  How to Uncover Expert Information on Any Subject</u>.  New
    York:  Harper & Row, 1987.
    How to do research with or without a library.

Gates, Jean K.  <u>Guide to the Use of Libraries and Information Sources</u>.  6th ed.  New York:
    McGraw-Hill, 1989.
    Describes the use of information sources in libraries and explains library
    organization.

Gelderman, Carol W.  <u>Better Writing for Professionals:  A Concise Guide</u>.  Glenview, IL:
    Scott, Foresman, 1984.

Hoel, Paul G. and Raymond J. Jessen.  <u>Basic Statistics for Business and Economics</u>.  2d ed.
    Santa Barbara, CA:  Wiley, 1977.
    Outlines the fundamentals of statistical theory necessary for solving management
    problems in business and government.

Huck, Schuyler W. , William G. Bounds, and William H. Cormier.  <u>Reading Statistics and
    Research</u>.  New York:  Harper & Row, 1974.
    A guide for those using statistics in research.

McCormick, Mona.  <u>The New York Times Guide to Reference Materials</u>.  rev. ed.  New
    York:  Times Books, 1985.
    Survey of standard works in various fields and tips on writing research papers.

C-1

Morris, Jacquelyn M. and Elizabeth A. Elkins. <u>Library Searching: Resources and Strategies</u>. New York: Jeffrey Norton, 1978.
Uses examples from the environmental sciences to illustrate basic search strategies.

Oppenheim, Abraham N. <u>Questionnaire Design and Attitude Measurement</u>. New York: Basic Books, 1966.
A definitive work in its field.

Rummel, J. Francis. <u>An Introduction to Research Procedures in Education.</u> 2d ed. New York: Harper & Row, 1964.
A practical guide to planning and organizing a research project; especially complete on questionnaire techniques.

Todd, Alden. <u>Finding Facts Fast: How to Find Out What You Want and Need to Know</u>. 2d ed. Berkeley, CA: Ten Speed Press, 1979.
A practical guide to efficient research.

Research Paper Format and Preparation

Campbell, William G., Carol Slade, and Stephen V. Ballou. <u>Form and Style: Theses, Reports, Term Papers.</u> 8th ed. Boston: Houghton Mifflin, 1990.
A succinct guide to the preparation of research papers.

<u>The Chicago Manual of Style</u>. 14th ed. Chicago: University of Chicago Press, 1993.
A definitive guide to the correct style and format of published materials.

Gibaldi, Joseph. <u>MLA Handbook for Writers of Research Papers / MLA Handbook</u>. 5th ed. New York: Modern Language Association of America, 1999.

Hodges, John C. <u>Harbrace College Handbook</u>. 13th ed. San Diego: Harcourt, Brace Jovanovich, 1998.
A comprehensive summary of the fundamentals of effective writing.

Hoemann, George H. <u>Electronic Style...the Final Frontier</u>. Updated 14 September 1998. Available [Online]:<<u>http://web.utk.edu/~hoemann/style.html</u>>[2 August 2000]

Matzen, Robert D. <u>Research Made Easy: A Guide for Students and Writers</u>. New York: Bantam, 1987.

C-2

A concise handbook containing basic research guidance as well as information on on-line services, rare book collections, etc.

Meyer, Michael. The Little, Brown Guide to Writing Research Papers. 3d ed. Boston: Little, Brown, 1994.

Morse, Grant W. Complete Guide to Organizing and Documenting Research Papers. New York: Fleet Academic Editions, 1974.
A. Though directed primarily at the college student, this book offers guidance on organizing and documenting material.

Page, Melvin. A Brief Citation Guide for Internet Sources in History and the Humanities. 20 February 1996. Available [Online]:<http://h-net2.msu.edu/~africa/citation.html>[2 August 2000].

Skillin, Marjorie, and Robert Malcolm Gay. Words into Type. 3d ed. Englewood Cliffs, NJ: Prentice-Hall, 1974.
A style manual which includes information on all aspects of the publication process.

Strunk, William, Jr. and E. B. White. The Elements of Style. 4th ed. Boston: Allyn and Bacon, 1999.
A concise guide to good, clear writing.

Sugden, Virginia M. The Graduate Thesis: The Complete Guide to Planning and Preparation. New York: Pitman, 1973.
Details the planning and development of an outline for doctoral dissertations, master's theses, and honors papers.

Turabian, Kate L. A Manual for Writers of Term Papers, Theses, and Dissertations, 6th ed., rev. by John Grossman and Alice Bennett. (Chicago: The University of Chicago Press, 1996).
A brief but standard guide to the preparation of research papers.

U.S. Government Printing Office. Style Manual. Washington, DC: 1984.
A standard reference for stylistic requirements of government publications.

Van Leunen, Mary-Claire. A Handbook for Scholars. rev. ed. New York: Oxford University Press, 1992.
How to write scholarly prose in an interesting and entertaining style.

C-3

Security and Copyright

U.S. Naval War College. Standard Organization and Regulations Manual July 2000. Available [Online]:http://nwcintranet/sorm/00sorm%20fm.pdf[4 August 2000] NWC mission, organizational structure, functions, policies and procedures and support relationships for Navy Warfare Development Command.

U.S. Secretary of the Navy Department of the Navy Information Security Program Regulation. SECNAVINST 5510.36. Naval policies and procedures for all matters of security.

C-4

# INDEX

I-1

I-2

Transmittal form 52-53
Treaty 24
Typing 4

## U

U.S. Code 23
U.S. Government document 20-23
U.S. Government document,
  periodical 24
U.S. or United States 7
Underlining 5
Underscoring 5
United Nations 24-25
United States or U.S.  7
Unpublished materials 30

## V

Verse quotations 6

## W

Warning notes 45
Word division 7
Word processing 4-8
Working papers 45
World Wide Web (WWW) 26

## X, Y, Z